THE LIFE HACK PLAYBOOK

The Life Hack Playbook

Proven Shortcuts to Peace & Purpose

Anne Karber

©2025 All Rights Reserved. No portion of this book may be reproduced, stored in a retrieval system, or transmitted in any form or by any means—electronic, mechanical, photocopy, recording, scanning, or other—except for brief quotations in critical reviews or articles without the prior permission of the author.

Published by Game Changer Publishing

Paperback ISBN: 978-1-969372-64-3

Hardcover ISBN: 978-1-969372-65-0

Digital ISBN: 978-1-969372-66-7

www.GameChangerPublishing.com

This book is dedicated to my Tribe of Ride or Dies.

To every soul who stood on the sidelines and cheered me on, even when it was hard to watch.

To those who saw the odds stacked against me, and still went all in.

This is my gift back to you—proof of scraped knees, cracked hearts, and the kind of stubborn MAD ASS faith that refuses to quit.

ADVANCE PRAISE

"*The Life Hack Playbook* completely transformed how I approach my daily routine. In just a few weeks, I felt more focused, less stressed, and surprisingly fulfilled. This book is a blueprint for anyone who wants to live smarter, not harder."

— Casey M.

"I've read a lot of self-help books, but none have been as actionable and down-to-earth as this one. The strategies are simple, yet the results are life-changing. It's like having a personal coach in your pocket."

— Belinda O.

"What I love about this book is that it doesn't overwhelm you with fluff—it gives you tools you can use today to feel better, think clearer, and live with intention. Highly recommended for anyone ready for a reset."

— Julio G.

"*The Life Hack Playbook* is a breath of fresh air. It helped me cut through the noise and find real peace in my everyday life. Each chapter felt like a conversation with a wise friend who truly gets it."

— Brennan W.

"This book isn't about hustle culture or unrealistic goals—it's about making small shifts that create massive impact. After reading it, I finally feel like I'm living on purpose, not just on autopilot."

— Cameron K.

"Every page of this book delivers insight, clarity, and encouragement. If you're feeling stuck or overwhelmed, this playbook will guide you back to what really matters—with ease."

— Tony W.

READ THIS FIRST

Just to say thanks for buying and reading my book,
I would like to connect with you!

Scan the QR Code Here:

THE & PROJECT

The world wants us divided. Politics, religion, race, gender, money
—you name it, there's a line drawn in the sand.
And every headline, every algorithm, every loud
voice is telling us to pick a side.

The & Project is my refusal to play that game.
The ampersand—**&**—is the symbol of connection. It says:
You & Me. This & That. Us & Them. Together. Not either/or,
not left or right, not black or white. Not us vs. them.

Both. All. Human
What began as a simple sticker with nothing but an ampersand has grown into a reminder: Unity is still possible. We can choose compassion over conflict. We can be wildly different and still stand next to each other without losing ourselves.

Healing starts small—one conversation, one moment, one brave decision to see another human being as more than a label. That's what the & stands for. That's the invitation inside this book: to live as a connector, not a divider.

So stick it. Share it. Live it.
Enough is enough. It's time to stop letting others profit from keeping us apart.

This is **The & Project**—and it starts with you.

DISCLAIMER

I'm not a therapist, life coach, or guru. I don't have a fancy degree, and I barely made it through high school without setting something on fire (metaphorically... mostly). What I do have is almost fifty years of real-life experience—complete with the highs, lows, wrong turns, late-night epiphanies, and more than a few "Ohhh... that's why that didn't work" moments.

This book isn't filled with clinical advice or science you can't pronounce. It's a collection of small, doable life hacks that have made a big difference for me and others who have earned a spot at my table of life. It's honest, a little scrappy, and totally judgment-free.

So no lab coat here—just coffee, a sense of humor, and some hard-earned wisdom. Take what resonates, leave what doesn't, and enjoy the ride.

PREFACE

This isn't the kind of book you breeze through and let collect dust on the shelf. It's a manual for hacking your own life. So grab a pen and a highlighter and actually use them as you're reading. Circle the stuff that punches you in the gut. Highlight the lines that make you laugh, or squirm, or want to throw the book across the room. Scribble in the margins like you're having an argument with me. I can take it.

And here's a pro move: If you start to feel defensive about something you read, don't brush it off. That's a giant neon arrow pointing right at the work you need to do. Make a note of it. Come back later when you're ready to get curious instead of reactive. That's where the good shit lives.

Keep a notebook handy, too. Jot down the hacks you want to try, the shifts you notice, and the "aha" moments you'll want to revisit when life inevitably gets messy again. That way, when you finish this book, you're not just closing a cover; you're walking away with a custom playbook built for your life. And when you need a refresher down the road (spoiler: you will), your own highlights and notes will point you right back to the tips and tricks worth adding into your mix.

THE LIFE HACK PLAYBOOK

PROVEN SHORTCUTS TO PEACE & PURPOSE

ANNE KARBER

FOREWORD

In a world that often feels like it's moving at a relentless pace, finding ways to simplify, streamline, and reclaim our time is more crucial than ever. Anne Karber's *The Life Hack Playbook* offers a refreshing approach to navigating the complexities of modern life. Drawing from her extensive experience in coaching and personal development, Anne provides practical strategies that empower individuals to take control of their daily routines and make intentional choices that align with their values.

What sets this playbook apart is its emphasis on actionable steps that can be seamlessly integrated into everyday life. Whether it's mastering time management, cultivating positive habits, or fostering meaningful connections, Anne's insights serve as a guide to living with purpose and authenticity. Her approach is rooted in the belief that small, consistent changes can lead to profound transformations.

As someone who has dedicated her career to helping others unlock their potential, Anne's voice resonates with clarity and

FOREWORD

compassion throughout this book. *The Life Hack Playbook* is not just a collection of tips and tricks; it's a roadmap to living a more intentional and fulfilling life.

—*Casey Morgan*

CONTENTS

Introduction	xxi
1. ENERGY = SKITTLES	**1**
Learning to See Energy	3
Overthinking Eats Up Your Skittles	4
Emotional Intelligence Is Energy Management	5
React vs. Respond: What's the Skittle Cost?	6
Moving Your Body Earns More Skittles	8
Everyday Skittle Multipliers	10
Currency and Cost	12
Skittles Inventory	13
Skittles Management and Protection	15
Top 10 Skittle Thieves	17
Top 10 Skittle Deposits	18
Challenge: Skittles Inventory	20
2. SAVAGE SELF-AWARENESS	**23**
Noise Is Cheap, Silence Pays Skittles	24
The Path to Self-Awareness	25
Don't Get Stuck With Old Beliefs	29
Challenge: Silence the Noise	30
3. FIX YOUR SHIT	**33**
You're Not Crazy, You've Been Conditioned	35
The Power of the Buffalo	37
Challenge: The Trigger Takedown	39
4. EQ = EMOTIONAL INTELLIGENCE	**41**
Master Your Emotions, Master the Game	45
Gut Check	47
Gut Rehab: Savage Edition	48
Challenge: EQ in Action	49
5. PERSPECTIVE	**51**
Every Choice Shapes Your Life	55
Challenge: Borrowed Lenses	59

6. MENTAL STRENGTH: STOP IT	61
Meet Your Psycho Roommate	62
Train Your Brain or It Trains You	68
Reclaim the Power That Was Always Yours	69
Challenge: Mastering Mental Strength	75
7. JUDGMENT	77
No More Petty, Only Progress	81
And Fellas…	82
Don't Compare, Celebrate Differences	84
Challenge: No Gossip, All Hype	88
8. STAY IN YOUR LANE	89
Stay in Your Lane to Find Your Peace	91
No Means No—For Everyone	96
Boundary Scripts to Steal	101
Challenge: Protect Your Lane	103
9. THE CUP	105
Fill Your Own Damn Cup	107
Challenge: Patch the Damn Cup	115
10. SETTING YOURSELF UP FOR SUCCESS	117
Habits Make or Break You	119
Challenge: Softball + Chill Way Combo	129
Conclusion	131
About the Author	137

INTRODUCTION

I have always been a lot. Since I was born, I have been a giant ball of energy. Looking back at pictures from when I was a little girl, the smile on my face was electric... literally magnetic. I always knew I was going to have a big life. I wasn't wrong. I have lived a **giant,** bold, and outrageous life.

I haven't done things perfectly and acknowledge the chaos. I think that's part of what makes what I have to say so important. I've lived... really lived. I've touched all the burners on the stove. I've done **all** the things. I've been messy AF and am on the other side to share the knowledge.

I wrestle with how much to say about who I am, because it's not what this book is about. I'd like to show you the receipts that I'm qualified and worth listening to, but I struggle with where to start and stop. Not from a place where I'm worried about being too vulnerable. I literally have a podcast that revolves around vulnerability... where I am the one leading with vulnerability to encourage others to do the same, so I've gotten quite comfortable showing the world the inside of my asshole. Not from a place where I'm worried about being judged. I don't give a flying fuck what people think. The reason that I wrestle is that there is way too much. I have taken every class offered at the University of Life—some more than once. I have my PhD from the School of Hard Knocks. I could give you all the facts and tell all the stories, but I'll save that for the book that has my picture on the front. What I will tell you is that I'm a successful woman by any measure. I have been in the trenches in life from all angles. I fought in the arena and won... marred and bloody, but victorious, nonetheless.

You should know that I barely graduated from high school. I don't have fancy degrees or training of any kind that make me qualified to give advice, therapist style. I grew up in a family of seven, with the opposite of money. I was a teenage mom. I didn't have a lot going for me. What I did have was that I am scrappy AF, gritty to my core, and relentless. I am fearless, and I'm not afraid to fail. I understand that failure is a part of the process and where we learn, so I know that I'm going to step up to the plate and swing for the fence every time.

Some people might ask how I started with nothing and got to where I am today. I clawed my way. I had faith that I could do anything... because I had no other option. I did a lot of cannonballing and figuring it out after I had already jumped. I was willing to do the hard thing... every time.

I didn't find success *despite* my scrappy beginnings; I found it *because* of them. Every setback, every hustle, and every lesson learned the hard way shaped my tenacity, resilience, and relentless drive to level up. I come from a background where nothing was handed to me, and I wouldn't have it any other way. That scrappiness built the foundation for the professional success I have today. I'm always evolving, always chasing growth, and always striving to be the most dialed-in version of myself, because when you come from the hustle, excellence isn't optional; it's a mindset.

INTRODUCTION

While I won't bore you with my story, I do find it important to set the stage for where my personal growth journey began. On October 29, 2016, I hit my rock bottom and made the life-altering decision to go to rehab and get sober. I was 39 years old and had spent the last several years of my drinking career really making a colossal mess of my life. Getting sober was a defining pivot point, one that changed everything.

For most of my life, I was in straight-up survival mode. I didn't process emotions; I buried them. Vulnerability wasn't even on my radar because I saw it as weakness. At that point, I had no grip on what I was feeling. My emotions were like wild raccoons in a trash can: chaotic, loud, and out of control... under the surface. On the surface, I looked calm, put together, even. But underneath, I was like a duck on a pond: gliding gracefully across the water while my feet paddled like hell just to stay afloat. That's what it felt like to live disconnected from my emotions, always hustling to hold it all together, terrified that if I slowed down or let anyone see the struggle, everything would come crashing down.

When I went to rehab, I thought that they were there to just keep the booze up on a higher shelf so I couldn't get to it until I dried out. Apparently, though, the rehab folks had other plans. They were there to help me figure out how to fix why I was drinking... to help me fix my shit. I found that I wasn't just drinking to run from the crushing grief of my sister's unexpected and tragic death. That was what eventually drove me over the edge, but I'd had a long history with alcohol. Booze and I were good friends... the best of friends. The incredible facilitators at the rehab were there to help me break up with alcohol for good. No forwarding address style.

I had been drinking to numb all the things that had happened when I was a child, all the things that had happened when I was a young adult, and all the things that had caused so much trauma in my life. I'd always thought, *It's fine... I'm fine... everything's fine.* Come to find out... it wasn't fine, I was not fine, and everything was so far from fine it was in a different area code.

Me getting sober was the start of healing forty years of bullshit. Clearing the wreckage started slowly. The first year was just trying to stay sober and work through putting the pieces of my life back together. My actions while I was still drinking took a serious toll on my family. The first year that I was sober was the hardest year of my life. I look back and literally wince at how much pain I experienced. I finally started to feel, really feel, and it *sucked*!

In the second year, I started to open my eyes a little bit. Life shifted, and I pivoted. All the while, I devoured self-improvement in every form or fashion that I could get my hands on. I grew curious about who Anne was and why she spent so much of her life creating distractions and numbing herself, unwilling to face the nasty, gross stuff that lived under the surface.

My journey started with baby steps, quiet, hesitant, but forward all the same. As I unearthed the trauma and tallied the ingredients in my recipe, I woke up to the truth: The work matters. With every layer I shed, the steps got bigger, bolder, and faster. And in the last few years, I've felt myself gathering unstoppable steam.

I have done so much therapy and consumed an obscene amount of personal growth books, podcasts, Reiki/energy work, breathwork, spiritual healing modalities, ayahuasca, other plant medicines, ceremonies, and healing connections with so many amazing people... **all** the things. When I can take what I've learned and put it into a straightforward, no-fluff format, it becomes approachable and has the power to create lasting change.

To me, there's no greater mission than the one I'm on right now. I've taken the high points and tools that worked in my life, run them through what I call the "ANNE filter," and distilled them

INTRODUCTION

into a clear, visual, and practical format, so you don't have to spend years turning your life into a self-help project. I've done the heavy lifting, breaking things down in a way that simplifies the hard stuff and makes it approachable, not overwhelming. And don't worry, I didn't just cook this up in my head and hope for the best. I've been testing it on my tribe for years, and the results speak for themselves. Around here, we joke that I'm batting a thousand... and the scoreboard is looking pretty damn good.

The "ANNE filter" didn't just shape this book; it's how I process everything for myself. It turns big, complex ideas into small, actionable steps that feel doable. And the best part? It works. The people I've shared it with have been able to take these concepts and apply them in ways that make real, lasting change.

You don't need to overhaul your entire life to start seeing results. Just a step here or there is enough to build momentum. And once you feel that traction, it inspires you to keep going. I'm here to show you that while you can't control life, you *can* control how you do life. You can run it instead of letting it run you.

Life is hard... for *everyone*. But most people don't realize that. We assume others have it easier: people without money think wealth makes life effortless, and those struggling with their weight assume fit people have it easy. But here's the truth: *All of it is hard.* Making money is hard. Being broke is hard. Taking care of your health is hard. Living in a body that feels like it's working against you is also hard.

You don't get to escape "hard," but you do get to choose your hard. So, stop wasting time comparing your struggle to someone else's highlight reel. No one gets a free pass. You have a choice: Stay stuck in victim mode or take the wheel and run your own damn race.

You have the power to write your own story; you're not stuck playing the hand you were dealt. That, to me, is incredibly powerful. Yes, it's hard. But you get to choose *your* version of hard. And yes, it takes work, but you're capable of doing it.

We've been grinding through life using outdated mindsets and strategies. Real growth comes from surrendering to what you can't control, getting your mind in check, and learning how to stop letting your thoughts run the show. That's where everything changes, individually and collectively.

My mission is to help you start doing the *right* kind of work, the work on yourself. We spend so much time and energy grinding for things that hold little real value, while the most important work, the inner work, gets pushed aside. But that's the work that truly changes everything.

That's what drives me to share what I've learned. I've spent years—*and more money than I care to admit*—digging through countless personal growth resources. But what I've found is this: It doesn't have to be that complicated. I've pulled the gold from all that work and turned it into tools and life hacks that help people unlock their potential, and I've watched it work time and time again.

I choose to lead with vulnerability because it's the only thing that cuts through the bullshit, and because I believe it opens the door for others to do the same. When we show up authentically and share who we really are, we create space for others to step into their truth, too. That's powerful.

All I'm asking is that you stay open. Be willing to get curious about yourself as you read or listen to this book. Let the ideas sink in, and explore how they relate to your life, your patterns, and your perspective.

Look at yourself not with judgment, but with curiosity. Be willing to get quiet. Be willing to sit in the discomfort. Because that's where growth lives, on the other side of honesty, reflection, and real self-awareness.

INTRODUCTION

It's exciting work! It's better than anything that they put out on TV or that you'll find at the bar. As you start doing the work, you'll peel back layers like an onion, and I highly recommend that you journal throughout the process so that you can go back and see how far you've come. It blows my mind every single time I go back and read an earlier entry.

Note: I'm not interested in judgment... either giving or receiving. If there is anything that you read in the following pages that feels like I'm coming from a judgy place, please know that that is not my intention. I have been in the trenches in this life and truly believe that there isn't one among us who has any business judging anyone else.

I have these life hacks to share because I've been through it and have the scars to show for it. If you find yourself feeling judgy as you're reading this, maybe consider getting curious about that, as that's about you, not me.

Happy reading!

CHAPTER 1
ENERGY = SKITTLES

I believe that energy is our biggest resource. Not money, not time, but energy. I also believe that most of us don't use this resource with intention or to its fullest potential. For years, I charged through life like an over-caffeinated squirrel without realizing I was burning through my stash. I had plenty of energy, but I spent it like a toddler armed with glitter... everywhere and on everyone. I never stopped to think about protecting it or using it wisely.

As I've been digging into my own growth, I've come face-to-face with the truth that energy is everything. Learning how to picture it, manage it, and work with it has flipped my world upside down in the best way. What's even more powerful is how this base understanding ripples into every corner of life.

I didn't pluck Skittles out of thin air. It took three forces colliding like a demolition derby to smash this thing into existence. And what came out of it? A visualization that's about to torch the rulebook and change the game for good.

1. Personal growth books that gave me the vocabulary
2. My friends' dream
3. My smart-ass niece and her silly prank

I was having lunch with a close friend of mine, and she was telling me a story about a dream she had. In that dream, I came to her and brought her energy. She said that the best way she could describe the image was me bringing little balls in my cupped hands. She described the little balls of energy like M&M's, for lack of better words. So, I had this image of my hands full of M&M's—my hands full of energy. I had been devouring personal growth books for the past eight years, and the concept of energy was at the core of the books I was reading at that time. I just didn't have the visualization yet. That is the part that always makes it more tangible for me. Books gave me the theory, but that image gave me the weapon.

A few weeks later, I was in Colorado hanging out with my brother and his family. We were playing cards, and I was explaining energy to them, as I understood it from my rapidly growing knowledge. I had a small bowl of Skittles that I was snacking on. As I was explaining energy to them, the Skittles in the bowl reminded me of my friend at lunch, telling me about her dream. The Skittles as energy was a way better visual for me because I'm not a chocolate fan, but I **love love love** Skittles.

The other thing that happened around the table that night that needs to be mentioned is that my niece, Josie, was messing with me, playing a prank on her Auntie. I kept thinking that I would be getting down to the end of the Skittles as I was enjoying them. We'd play a few rounds of cards, and I'd look down, and there were quite a bit more Skittles than I remembered. I was the only one eating out of that bowl, so the Skittles quantity fluctuation had me scratching my head. They all delivered lies with the composure of Oscar-winning actors when I asked if someone was messing with me. This went on the entire evening. I would get low on Skittles, we would play a few rounds of cards, or I would get up to use the restroom, and by the time I got my hand back into the bowl, it would be heavier than how I recall leaving it. I couldn't figure out what was happening. I started envisioning the story of Jesus and the fishes, and I was thinking that I was witnessing a modern-day version, only with Skittles. It wasn't until weeks later that my family fessed up. It was hilarious! From that day forward, Skittles as energy has been seared into my brain.

LEARNING TO SEE ENERGY

Over the last several years, I've dived headfirst into understanding this mysterious force we call "energy." I learned to visualize it, talk about it, and even measure it in my own quirky way. Energy became Skittles—bright, countable, and playful enough to turn something abstract into something I could work with.

Being a visual learner, I need to see it to get it. Otherwise, abstract concepts set up camp in the "lost and found" section of my brain. Michael Singer's *The Untethered Soul* was my gateway drug—it showed me how to take intangible things swirling in my head and give them shape. I ran with that idea like a kid at recess, applying visualization to everything in my life. It was an Oprah "aha" moment on steroids.

As I realized the power of energy, the Skittles image brought it to life. It was fun; it was quantifiable; and it turned energy into a game. I could feel each one slip away or land in my bowl. Suddenly, I knew when I was overflowing and when I was scraping the bottom—and more importantly, I could link those states directly to my choices. Whenever my bowl was empty at night, I knew my Skittles had been tossed into black holes. That flipped a switch—I started protecting my energy like it was gold.

The analogy spread quickly. I shared it with friends, family, and eventually anyone within earshot. Watching the lightbulb moments as people suddenly *understood* that energy management was like hosting a game show and handing out prizes. Before long, people were telling me they were making wiser "Skittle" choices and seeing big improvements in every area of life. Who knew a candy analogy could be that powerful?

And the wild part: Beyoncé gets the same amount of Skittles. Oprah? Same. Nobody gets bonus candy, no matter how shiny their title. That realization was both hilarious and empowering.

There are plenty of ways to drain your stash and plenty of ways to fill it back up. Being mindful to understand your balance is critical.

OVERTHINKING EATS UP YOUR SKITTLES

Think about a time when your brain just would not shut up, rehashing a tough situation, overthinking every scenario, or beating yourself up about something you said or did. You end up drained, exhausted, like your own mind has been joyriding you around all day without your permission. Every mental loop has a Skittles price tag. It's basically the world's shittiest streaming service; your brain keeps auto-playing reruns you didn't subscribe to, with no skip button. And every time you watch the same episode again, more Skittles disappear from your stash. Total waste of candy.

Pattern Interrupt: The next time you catch your brain hitting "replay," literally say out loud (or in your head if you're in public): "Not paying Skittles for this rerun." Then swap the channel. Call a friend, blast a song that makes you move, or redirect into something that gives you a Skittles deposit. The goal isn't to stop thoughts completely (spoiler: that doesn't work), it's to stop *funding* them.

A looming decision, nonstop work stress, friend drama, worry about someone you love—every one of them eats Skittles. The hamster wheel isn't free; it bleeds you dry. If you choose to mindfuck yourself over what you can't control, fine. But don't whine when you've got nothing left.

Have you ever replayed a conversation in your head countless times and imagined dozens of alternate endings? You just dumped half your bowl of Skittles onto the ground. How about mentally composing an email in the shower, rewriting it in the car, and then never sending it because you lost your nerve? Yep, more Skittles down the drain. Our minds are drama factories, churning out imaginary arguments with strangers, hypothetical scenarios that never happen, and highlight reels of every embarrassing thing we've ever done. Each mental rerun costs candy. Once you realize that every epic mental saga is coming out of your daily Skittles budget, you'll think twice about binge-watching your own thoughts.

Most of us burn up a ton of energy replaying past events in our minds. The past is for learning from, not for living in. Take the lesson, then let it go. Picture tying it to a helium balloon and releasing it into the sky.

EMOTIONAL INTELLIGENCE IS ENERGY MANAGEMENT

Emotions are another big Skittles cost. If your emotional intelligence is underdeveloped (and don't worry—most of us are basically still in remedial classes here), you'll burn through your stash by *reacting* instead of *responding*.

Here's the difference: Reacting is knee-jerk. It's snapping, sulking, yelling, or shutting down without a single thought—basically torching your candy bowl just because someone breathed wrong. Responding is different. It's strategic. It's the pause before the strike, the breath before the choice, the moment you guard your Skittles instead of hemorrhaging them.

REACT VS. RESPOND: WHAT'S THE SKITTLE COST?

Scenario	React (Drain)	Respond (Deposit/Save)
Someone cuts you off in traffic	Yell, flip them off, stew for 30 minutes	Take a deep breath, turn up your playlist
Your partner forgets to do something	Snap, sulk, cold-shoulder	Calmly remind them or ask for what you need
A coworker takes credit for your idea	Gossip, passive-aggressively withdraw	Direct convo: "Hey, I'd like credit for that."
Your kid spills juice on the carpet	Freak out, lecture for 15 minutes	Laugh, grab a towel, teach cleanup skills
Your friend cancels plans last minute	Spiral into "nobody values me" mode	Use the time for a deposit activity you enjoy

Reacting almost always costs you *more* than you think. Responding almost always saves or adds Skittles you didn't realize you could keep. Reacting often costs you triple because you pay in the moment *and* later when you replay it in your head or clean up the mess it caused. Responding, however, is like coupon-clipping—you acknowledge the feeling, validate it, and spend only what's necessary, often getting some Skittles back in the process.

The more you practice, the less you bleed Skittles on unnecessary drama, and the more you have available for joy, creativity, and the stuff that lights you up.

My favorite example of someone wasting Skittles in a big way is the big-truck guy in traffic who loses his mind over absolutely nothing. Traffic happens. How this is still shocking to people amazes me. Think about this guy: He can't handle being cut off or someone driving five miles per hour under the speed limit. He's pounding his steering wheel, honking, and hurling Skittles out the window like Mardi Gras beads. All because he can't handle something that happens every single day. Doesn't that sound ridiculous? I'm continually fascinated by people who act like regular life is a personal affront to them.

Since we've mentioned the big-truck guy, let's identify some of the other characters who snack on your Skittles. There's the grocery store aisle blocker who parks their cart right in front of the exact cereal you need while they read the ingredient list on every box. There's the couple at the movie theater who whisper loudly during the film. There's your coworker who always has a catastrophe that somehow becomes your problem. Each one of these everyday villains offers a chance to practice keeping your candy. Laugh at the absurdity, smile at the drama, and picture yourself saving Skittles for something worthwhile—like tackling a passion project, crushing a workout, laughing with friends, or sinking into a long bath.

When you're going through something emotional, it drains you. After a heavy day of feelings, I feel like I've gone a few rounds in the ring. Losing a pet, ending a relationship, getting laid off—those are big-ticket Skittle expenses. Knowing that makes me want to spend wisely, not scatter them willy-nilly. Save your emotional Skittles for the real stuff so you can really process it, instead of stuffing it down and layering Netflix, booze, or busyness on top. That's a thief of joy. Stop it.

Ever dealt with something emotional and felt like you got run over by a truck afterward? Yeah—me too. If I cry, like really ugly cry, I'm toast for the day. Honestly, even if I just leak a tear or two, I'm wiped. For years, I didn't process emotions at all, and it wrecked me. Worth the work I've put in since, but it was *rough AF*.

So why do emotions feel like a full-body workout with no endorphin rush? Because there's a Skittles cost. That realization is what pushed me toward building emotional intelligence—EQ for short. And no, EQ isn't some mystical PhD thing or an algebra formula. It's simply your ability to notice, understand, and manage your own emotions (and other people's) without losing your damn Skittles.

Most of us weren't handed an EQ manual growing up. We're out here trying to adult with the emotional toolkit of a middle-schooler—think slamming doors, sulking, or ghosting people instead of communicating. But EQ is like finally learning to use the real tools of adulthood. It's the difference between pounding a screw into the wall with your shoe versus grabbing the right screwdriver and fixing it in seconds. Once you learn it, life just works better.

Low EQ is like driving around on bald tires—eventually you skid out and wonder why everything feels like a crash. Building EQ is like finally putting good tread on: you've got traction, control, and you're not burning through Skittles every mile. And trust me, the investment pays off everywhere in life.

MOVING YOUR BODY EARNS MORE SKITTLES

Physical exertion also costs Skittles. The good news? Many physical expenditures come with a great return on investment. Exercising, dancing, or moving your body generally gives you more candy back. Picture how great you feel after a dance break; it's like a Skittle dividend.

Pro Tip: Dancing should be part of your daily routine. Squeeze it in while brushing your teeth, making coffee, or walking the dog. Sing, dance, and enjoy the mundane. It's a life hack because you'll reap way more Skittles than you spend. Don't worry about being a good dancer. You're not auditioning for *So You Think You Can Dance*. No one's watching, and if they are, they can always change the channel if they don't like your vibe. We're meant to move, laugh, and not take ourselves so seriously. Dancing brings out all the good stuff we're trying to cultivate. And if you're a guy thinking, *Yeah, dancing's not my thing,* cool. Blast music in the garage, shadow-box for a round, chest-bump the air like you scored the winning touchdown, or just head-bang like you're at a Metallica concert. Same Skittles return, zero rhythm required.

And that's the thing about movement—it doesn't just shift your body, it shifts your energy. So let's stay on this groove and talk about the ROI on physical Skittles. When you move your body in a way that feels good, it's like an instant candy rebate. You could do squats until your legs burn, run around the block, or twirl in your living room—your choice. Even mundane tasks can become mini workouts. Do calf raises while you brush your teeth. Bust out a few lunges while you're waiting for your coffee to brew. Take a silly victory lap around the kitchen after you empty the dishwasher. These micro movements don't just help your body; they feed your Skittles jar. They remind you that exercise doesn't have to be a punishment. It can be a celebration of being alive.

When you think about the Skittles cost of physical exertion, it's important to realize that while movement does spend energy, it usually cycles it right back—and often with interest. Exercise, play, and movement aren't draining obligations; they're Skittle multipliers. Think about when you crank up the music and start dancing.

Nothing starts free; even momentum charges a cover. But if you're anything like me, a few songs of kitchen dancing with your kids—laughing, being silly, totally letting loose, actually leaves you more energized than when you started. That's not just exercise; that's a candy deposit disguised as fun.

EVERYDAY SKITTLE MULTIPLIERS

- **Walking outside.** Costs a handful, gives back double when the fresh air clears your head.
- **Playing catch with your kid.** Burns a little, but the joy on their face is a jackpot deposit.
- **Playing with your pet.** Tossing the ball, tug-of-war, or belly rubs—minimal cost, massive Skittle return from unconditional love.
- **Stretching in the morning.** Tiny effort, big payoff in clarity and focus.
- **Throwing weights around.** Costs a chunk, but the endorphins pay you back like interest on steroids.
- **Cleaning with music on.** Sure, chores cost energy, but pair them with a dance party and you come out ahead.
- **Gardening or tinkering.** Whether it's dirt under your nails or tools in the garage, creating something fuels you back up.
- **Pickup sports with friends.** Basketball, soccer, flag football—burns plenty, but competition + camaraderie = Skittle gold.
- **Yoga, breathwork, or martial arts.** Costs a few Skittles to start but multiplies calm, focus, strength, and balance.

- **Laugh-out-loud play.** Tag, Nerf war, pillow fight, or inside jokes that have you wheezing—laughter supercharges your energy bank.
- **Hiking, biking, or fishing.** Burns calories and Skittles but refills your bowl with joy, adventure, and peace.
- **Swimming.** Full-body cost, but the water itself is like plugging your bowl into a charger.
- **Grilling out.** Costs a few Skittles to fire it up, but the flavor and good company pay you back in spades.
- **Cold plunge or ice shower.** Costs every Skittle you think you have, but refills your bowl with grit, clarity, and swagger.
- **Sex.** *Big* Skittle payoff when done with the right person and energy.

Important to Note: Not all physical activity is a multiplier—dragging yourself to do something you hate (like a workout that feels like punishment) usually just drains you. The trick is finding movement that feels good to *you*. That's where the deposits live.

Working out isn't just about six-pack abs and Instagram flexes. It's about energy management. Physical movement is one of the fastest ways to deposit Skittles back into your bowl. Think of exercise as a candy multiplier: You spend a few Skittles to get moving, but the payoff is always more than you invested, by a mile.

When you sweat, stretch, or just shake it out in your living room, you're not only boosting your body battery, you're clearing out mental clutter and emotional sludge, too. It's like hitting the refresh button on all three levels: brain, heart, and body.

And the best part? It doesn't have to look like a hardcore gym session. A walk around the block, air-drumming in your car, yoga in your pajamas—it all counts. The goal isn't perfection; the goal is movement. Every step, squat, or shimmy is a deposit. The more you move, the more Skittles you have to play with in every other part of your life.

So next time you're debating whether to work out, picture yourself sliding Skittles back into your bowl, one rep, one laugh, one drop of sweat at a time. Energy in, candy up.

CURRENCY AND COST

Imagine your Skittles as a currency. If you can learn to manage it, you're not just budgeting for bills, you're budgeting for joy. Think zero-based budgeting: every dollar has a job before the month begins. Same with your Skittles. Allocate some for essentials like work and family, set aside a stash for self-care, and keep a little emergency fund for when life throws a tantrum, a flat tire, a forgotten password, or a toddler meltdown (performed either by you or your actual toddler). With a plan, you won't have to borrow from tomorrow's stash. Just like financial health, energy health requires boundaries, intention, and the occasional audit.

You already know the people and activities that refill your bowl. Do more of those. And you definitely know the ones that leave you feeling mugged and empty. Do less of those. Start watching yourself spend Skittles. Literally picture it. It's hilarious and sobering when you realize how many you've thrown away without even noticing. And one of the biggest hidden drains? Emotions. Anger especially.

Anger itself isn't the enemy; it's just energy with a message, your internal warning light saying: *Hey, something's not okay here.* Ignore it, and you torch your stash without learning the lesson. Acknowledge it, express it constructively, and you keep your candy.

Once I started treating everyday annoyances as a Skittles experiment, everything shifted. Slow Wi-Fi, the guy arguing in the checkout line, the spilled coffee, the lost keys—all of them give me the same choice: do I toss Skittles at the irritation, or do I save them for something that actually matters? It's always either/or. Blow your stash on petty stuff and you're drained. Save it for playing catch with your kid, laughing with friends, or doing something that fuels you, and you walk away richer.

So, ask yourself: *Who and what am I spending Skittles on? Who fills my bowl, and who empties it?* If you're a people-pleaser, this will be huge—you've probably been handing out Skittles like Costco samples for a long time. But once you start tracking the real cost, you can stop sleepwalking through old patterns and start making deliberate trades.

It really is that simple: Everything is a choice. Blow your stash on road rage and petty complaints, or protect it like the priceless treasure it is. What would it look like if your family, your passions, and *you* got your Skittles instead of the lady at Starbucks cutting in line?

The more curious you get about your Skittle spending, the more powerful you become. You start breaking patterns that never served you in the first place, and you realize you're not here to live the same mediocre day on repeat. You're here to enjoy the ride. And once you see the Skittle price tag, you'll never unsee it.

SKITTLES INVENTORY

Your energy is yours, and yours alone, to decide how you spend. Nobody else gets to swipe your candy card without your permission. The trick is developing a savage self-awareness of where your Skittles are going. Once you see the leaks, you can plug them. Once you see the drains, you can swap them out for deposits. That's where the game begins: Trade the things that empty your bowl for things that fill it up.

Start by running an inventory. Where are your Skittles drains? Obligations? Emotional hostage situations? The things you keep saying yes to, even though every fiber of your being is screaming no? Be honest here. It's not about ditching every responsibility; life has non-negotiables, but it *is* about calling out the nonsense you've been programmed to tolerate. Most of us are running on defective cultural software. We say yes so people won't judge us, we overextend ourselves because we think we're supposed to, and we pretend that martyrdom is noble. No one wins in that equation. Not you, not them. So why do we keep doing it? Time to hit "update software."

When you strip away the obligations that don't belong to you, you don't just save Skittles, you overflow. You find yourself sitting on a full bowl, with plenty to share from a place of abundance rather than resentment. And when you give from abundance, the people in your life get the *best* version of you, not the drained, bitter, keep-score version.

This is the download I hope lodges in your brain and never lets go. Doing this work might feel counterintuitive, prioritizing your happiness over your partner's, your kids', or anyone else's. But it's exactly what needs to happen if you want to stop existing and start genuinely living. When you choose what makes *you* happy, you end up showing up as a fuller, brighter, more magnetic human, and everyone around you benefits.

I know this because I've lived both lives. In my old chapter, I was buried under obligations, running on resentment, and constantly in Skittle debt. Then I got ruthless. I adopted a savage self-awareness and started making consistent, often uncomfortable choices that prioritized me. *What did I want? What made me feel alive?* Once I answered those questions and adjusted my life accordingly, I became a version of Anne that my past self couldn't have even dreamed up. And if you ask anyone in my life today, they'll tell you the same thing: I'm better for them than I ever was back when I was drowning in "shoulds."

So grab your metaphorical clipboard and do your Skittles inventory. Track the leaks. Audit the drains. And then get curious: What would it look like to stop handing out free samples of your candy to anyone who asks and instead stockpile enough Skittles to build a life you truly love?

SKITTLES MANAGEMENT AND PROTECTION

Once you realize Skittles are your currency, the next step is learning to manage and protect them like your life depends on it, because it does. Energy isn't infinite. You get a bowl in the morning, and that's it. How you spend, save, and protect it determines whether you collapse into bed running on fumes or still have energy left in the tank.

Management looks like planning ahead, setting boundaries, and making conscious trades instead of emotional impulse buys. Think of it like meal-prepping for your candy: You allocate Skittles where they'll matter most instead of blowing them all by noon on stress, people-pleasing, and traffic tantrums.

Protection, on the other hand, is about guarding your stash from Skittle thieves. These are the people, situations, and habits that sneak in and steal candy while you're not looking. The complainer at work. The toxic family member who thrives on drama. The endless doomscrolling at 11 p.m. Every time you let them in without a filter, they're picking Skittles out of your bowl.

Here are a few rules of Skittle management and protection:

1. **Budget your Skittles.** Start the day knowing roughly where you want them to go. Work, family, self-care, fun. If everything is "essential," nothing is. Prioritize.

2. **Set boundaries = lock your candy jar.** Saying no isn't rude; it's protective. You wouldn't leave your wallet on the counter at a gas station. Stop leaving your Skittles unattended with people who drain you.
3. **Identify the Skittle thieves.** Energy vampires, toxic groups, habits that leave you empty. Make a list. Awareness alone changes the game.
4. **Invest in Skittle multipliers.** Exercise, laughter, sleep, deep conversations, creativity. These don't just save Skittles; they pay you back with interest.
5. **Do random audits.** Stop mid-week and ask: *Where's my bowl at? Am I spending wisely, or tossing Skittles into black holes?* Audit often enough, and you'll naturally course-correct.

Managing and protecting your Skittles doesn't make you selfish. It makes you effective. You can't help your people, crush your goals, or enjoy your damn life if you're running on empty. Protecting your Skittles is the most generous thing you can do, because when you're full, everybody around you gets the best of you.

So guard your stash. Spend it wisely. And remember: Skittles aren't unlimited, but with the right management, you'll always have enough for what really matters.

Ready to see where your Skittles vanish—and how to win them back? Let's call out the thieves before we stack the deposits.

TOP 10 SKITTLE THIEVES

1. **Traffic Tantrums.** Losing your cool over brake lights is like setting your Skittles on fire. Spoiler: the freeway doesn't care.
2. **Weather Complaints.** Fighting the weather won't fix it—each gripe costs you candy you'll never get back.
3. **Overcommitment.** Saying *yes* when you want to say "hell no." Congratulations, you just donated Skittles to the guilt bank.
4. **People-Pleasing.** Handing out Skittles like free Costco samples to everyone but yourself.
5. **Gossip & Drama.** Nothing empties your bowl faster than marinating in someone else's soap opera.
6. **Doomscrolling.** Social media = Skittles slot machine. Pull the lever, lose candy, repeat.
7. **Unfinished Conversations.** That thing you should've said but didn't? It'll loop in your head until it costs you double.
8. **Comparison Games.** Measuring your bowl against Beyoncé's. Reminder: she has the same number of Skittles.
9. **Resentment Hoarding.** Holding grudges like a collector's item. They depreciate fast and drain your stash.
10. **Crappy sleep.** Staying up late for "just one more episode." Nothing robs tomorrow's bowl faster than robbing yourself of rest.

Pro Tip: Awareness is half the battle. Once you can spot the thieves, you can stop leaving your candy jar unlocked.

TOP 10 SKITTLE DEPOSITS

1. **Deep Sleep.** The original candy factory. Eight hours = a Skittle jackpot.
2. **Laughter.** Belly laughs with people who get you are like dropping a whole bag back in your bowl.
3. **Movement.** Doesn't matter if it's yoga, squats, or a kitchen dance party. Move your body, earn your candy.
4. **Quality Time.** With people who light you up, not drain you. Bonus if it involves connection without screens.
5. **Nature Fix.** A walk, a hike, or just sitting under a tree. The outdoors is a Skittle multiplier.
6. **Creativity.** Writing, painting, building, singing—making stuff puts deposits straight into your Skittle savings account.
7. **Acts of Service (when chosen, not obligated).** Helping out because you *want* to, not because you *have* to. Huge candy boost.
8. **Gratitude Practice.** Stopping to notice the good stuff is like finding Skittles you didn't know you had.
9. **Play.** Board games, sports, pillow fights, Nerf wars—fun without an agenda refills your stash fast.
10. **Stillness.** Meditation, breathing, or just sitting quietly with your coffee. Sometimes the best deposit is simply not spending at all.

Pro Tip: Stack your deposits. For example, go for a walk with a friend who makes you laugh = nature + connection + laughter. That's a triple Skittle win.

THE LIFE HACK PLAYBOOK

Managing your Skittles isn't just about energy; it's about taking back your life. Every excuse your mind throws up, every obligation you never even signed up for, every "good girl" pattern you've been programmed with... those are drains. And the cost is steep. You end up resentful, exhausted, and empty, wondering why you're carrying everyone else's laundry basket when nobody asked you to in the first place.

Brutal truth: No one asked you to. And you don't have to keep doing it.

I learned the hard way that I'd spent years living like a martyr, overworked, overstressed, and over everything. Then my husband asked me a simple question that knocked me flat: *"Who asked you to?"* That moment cracked me open. I realized I was choosing resentment and depletion by trying to hold everything together for everyone else. Once I stopped, not only did my bowl fill up, but my husband, my kids, my friends, and everyone around me got the best version of me. Turns out no one wanted my resentful energy disguised as "help" anyway.

When you protect your Skittles and put your mask on first, everyone benefits. Your kids get a parent who's present instead of fried. Your partner gets a teammate instead of a martyr. Your friends get laughter instead of leftovers. You get to live instead of resent.

The real magic? It's not about giant life overhauls. It's about tiny hacks. Buy the cushy bike seat. Teach your kids to do their own laundry. Stop saying you "don't have time" and start admitting when you simply didn't make something a priority. Start swapping out Skittle drains for Skittle deposits until your bowl is overflowing.

And don't forget your eight-year-old self. That version of you knew how to laugh, play, and find joy in simple things like bike rides, eating watermelon or an ice cream cone on a hot day, running in the sun, or maybe even petting snakes. That's the self you need to invite back into your life, because those moments are energy multipliers. They light you up. They refill your bowl.

So here's your invitation: slow down, get curious, and start playing the Skittles game. Audit your drains. Protect your stash. Make the swaps. Do more of what feels like freedom and less of what feels like obligation. Because once you see energy this way, once you feel it, once you know it, you can't unknow it.

I'm telling you, this is the life hack of all life hacks. Skittles are energy. Energy is life. Keep your bowl full, and watch how everything changes.

CHALLENGE: SKITTLES INVENTORY

Grab a notebook, open your notes app, or scribble on a napkin—I don't care where, just get it down. Time to see where your Skittles are really going.

Step 1: List the Drains

- Who or what leaves you feeling like you got mugged in a back alley—empty bowl, zero Skittles?
- Which obligations feel like emotional hostage situations?
- Where are you saying *yes* when your whole body wants to scream, "hell no"?
- Bonus: Write down the stuff you complain about on repeat. (Hint: that's a drain.)

Step 2: List the Deposits

- Who makes you feel energized, happy, or proud of yourself after you spend time with them?
- What activities light you up and leave you overflowing instead of depleted?
- Where do you feel most like *you*—creative, playful, relaxed, or powerful?

Step 3: Run the Math

- Look at your drains list. Which ones are true non-negotiables (a.k.a. adulting)? Which ones are outdated "shoulds" you can let go of?
- Look at your deposits list. How can you swap in more of these and crowd out the drains?
- If each drain cost you ten Skittles and each deposit gave you ten back, how would your current balance sheet look? Be honest.

Step 4: Make the Trade

- Pick one drain you're going to cut, reduce, or reframe.
- Pick one deposit you're going to add more of this week.
- That's it. One trade at a time. Small swaps, big impact.

Pro Tip: Repeat this inventory often. Just like money, your Skittles flow changes with the season you're in. Keep auditing, keep adjusting, and you'll build a candy-rich life instead of running in debt.

Final "Energy = Skittles" Thought: **Now that you visualize energy this way, you can't unsee it. It will be like a song that you can't get out of your head. Sorry, not sorry!**

Welcome to the Skittles gang!

CHAPTER 2
SAVAGE SELF-AWARENESS

Self-awareness is where change starts—period. You can't fix what you won't face. Most people would rather cling to their bullshit than admit they're the problem. They guard their version of reality like it's sacred, even when it's wrecking them. But if you've got the guts to actually look in the mirror, everything changes.

I lacked self-awareness in my previous life and had my ego on a steady diet of bullshit and bravado. I thought the world revolved around me, and everyone else was just living in my story. I put up walls to prevent deep, meaningful connections. I didn't know any other way or that things could be so much better. Knowing better changed everything for me, and now I'm here to pass the playbook so you can break free and build a life that blows your old one out of the water.

While you may read this and think that you are already self-aware, I encourage you to really dive in from a fresh perspective. I learned the hard way that what I *thought* was self-awareness was just the tip of the iceberg. You're the one who cashes in on this work. More clarity, more energy, more peace. So don't half-ass it—get curious and find the blind spots you've been ignoring.

NOISE IS CHEAP, SILENCE PAYS SKITTLES

You start by being willing to get quiet. And I don't mean monk-on-a-mountain quiet—I mean creating even a sliver of space where the noise of life isn't running the show. No podcasts blasting, no texts lighting up your phone, no endless to-do list screaming at you. Just you, your thoughts, and maybe the sound of your own breathing. At first, it feels awkward, even uncomfortable, because your brain will throw everything at you—random grocery lists, old conversations, the itch to grab your phone. Let it. That's your mind unclogging the pipes. If you stick with it, past the static, that's where the good stuff shows up: your real thoughts, your gut instincts, the truth you usually drown out. Quiet isn't empty. Quiet is where your self-awareness finally has room to speak.

Getting quiet is the doorway. Once you've made space for your own thoughts to surface, the next step is learning how to stay present with them. That's where mindfulness comes in. Mindfulness means being *present* and *aware* in your own life. It's paying attention—on purpose—to what you're doing, how you're feeling, and what it's costing you. When you're mindful, you stop running on autopilot. You stop burning through your Skittles without realizing where they're going. You *notice* what's draining you and what's filling you up. You get intentional instead of reactive. Strategic instead of scattered.

Mindfulness is about noticing. Reflection is about recording. When you put the two together, you start seeing patterns you'd never catch in the daily chaos. If you don't already have a journaling practice, I **highly** recommend that you start one. You can do that by writing in an actual notebook, on a computer or laptop, in the notes app of your phone, or in any other way that resonates with you. If you've struggled in the past to get something to stick, throw out any rules or limiting beliefs. It can look like whatever you want it to look like. There are no rules.

I had a mental roadblock to journaling after my trust was compromised when I was a child. It felt like a violation to me. I spent decades not journaling. A few years back, a mentor of mine suggested that I buy a small safe to store my journal so I would have the outlet without worrying that someone else would read my most intimate thoughts and feelings. That investment of ninety-nine dollars and a different perspective made all the difference for me. Quick life hack if you've got the same privacy hangup: Give yourself permission to create a safe space—literally. Whether it's a lockbox, a hidden drawer, or a password-protected doc, the point isn't the container; it's giving your mind permission to unload without fear of being read. That little trick was the key that unlocked years of stuck thoughts for me.

So much growth has come out of my journaling practice. I'm obsessed with it; every day it teaches me more about myself. It's **way** better than anything I could watch on TV. Also, it's neat to be able to gauge my progress when I go back to prior entries to see where I was a year ago, two years ago, etc.

THE PATH TO SELF-AWARENESS

After you've had some time to get quiet, mindful, and reflective, you might be brave enough to wade into requesting an alternative perspective and/or constructive feedback from the people who've earned a place at your table of life. I won't lie; this part takes work. Letting people hold up a mirror to your blind spots isn't fun, but it is powerful. Their perspective helps you see the effect your actions have on others, and while it can be uncomfortable, it's also one of the fastest ways to grow.

After you take in feedback from your trusted circle, the next move is to face your own history. Your past is full of receipts, and digging through them shows you exactly how you became who you are today. That's the payoff of self-exploration—you stop guessing and start actually knowing what makes you tick. Instead of floating through life half-asleep, you get to chart your course toward the shit that matters, the stuff that makes you feel alive, and the impact you want to have.

Before I gained all the self-awareness that I now have (btw, that still grows every single day), I built my own cage by not engaging with other people in meaningful ways. When I got sober in 2016, it was a giant wake-up call for me.

I spent a month in rehab, and during that time, I attended a few AA meetings, which, initially, I wasn't very excited about going to. After going enough times to understand what AA was all about, it changed my life in a big way.

The 12-step program doesn't just suggest it—it demands you look in the mirror, take accountability, and own your shit. No excuses. The mirror doesn't lie; it shows you exactly who you are. The hardest person to figure out isn't your boss, your partner, or your friends. It's you. Savage self-awareness means having the guts to get curious about your own reflection, take accountability for what you see, and sit with whatever the hell it shows you.

After I had been working on myself for a few years, I came to a place where I was willing to listen to others about the impact that I had on their lives, which is also an extremely important part of AA's 12-step program. When you're consumed with yourself, you have little regard for what your actions bring to others in your life.

I was literally a tornado in the lives of the people doing life with me, and I didn't realize it. In getting curious about myself, I started to listen with as much passion as I wanted to be heard with, and I started journaling about what I found in the quiet.

I had trusted conversations with people I knew had my best interests at heart, and I was able to not be defensive when they told me things about myself that were hard to hear. That doesn't come naturally, by the way. It's something that takes work because we all have a pile of triggers and are so defensive about everything that we have a hard time being willing to hear the tough stuff.

When someone is willing to say the hard things, to help you look in the mirror, don't be defensive. Just listen and receive it, even if it stings. Sometimes you'll ask a friend for feedback and their answer won't be what you wanted to hear—that's the gold. It often takes a true "ride-or-die" friend to say the thing that will trigger the hell out of you, but they do it anyway because they love you enough to want what's best for you. Be grateful to them for showing up for you in a big way.

Generally, when someone tries to tell us something about ourselves, we end up cutting them off before they can finish. We get defensive right away. We try to justify whatever our actions were. But that's not necessary. Come at this from a place of curiosity. Leave judgment out of it and do everything you can not to get defensive. There's no place for either of those things here. They aren't productive and only get in the way of our growth.

You don't need to make excuses for anything. At this stage of self-awareness, you're just on a fact-finding mission to figure things out a little bit. You're just noticing at this point. Nothing else is required. If you listen, you will realize where there's work to be done.

Take stock of where you're happy with yourself and where you see room for growth. As you do, it's crucial to seek feedback from people who A: have earned a seat at your table of life, and/or B: are already where you're striving to be. They've walked the path ahead and know the terrain.

Be ruthless about who gets a say in your growth. Not every loudmouth deserves a microphone in your life. Feedback from people who don't understand the work you're doing, or who secretly want to see you fail, is toxic. That's not perspective; that's poison. Protect your process. Only listen to the ones in the arena, bleeding and sweating next to you. Couch critics and sideline spectators? They don't get a vote. If they're not adding value, their "advice" is just noise. And you don't owe noise any space.

We often give the wrong things too much mental space, and that clutters the path to healing and happiness. Letting negative, unhelpful thoughts take up real estate in your mind can be more harmful than you realize, especially when you're trying to process, move forward, and evolve.

As you're going through the self-awareness component, you will be challenged to look at everything. You will come across things that you didn't even realize you were carrying around or doing. You will become aware of things that you don't love and don't want to carry forward. You will come across things that are hard to look at, things that are character defects, or things that you don't even know where they came from.

Go through this exploration without judgment because it doesn't matter where the parts and pieces came from that make you who you currently are. This step in the process is just taking inventory. You may figure out later where things started, or you may not, but just staying open to discovering everything, good and bad, is the most important component of this process.

What do you like? What do you not like? You can't fix what's hiding in plain sight. For me, one of the most eye-opening parts of this process was realizing how many limiting beliefs were quietly steering my choices. The way through is curiosity. Get curious about yourself. Get curious about your triggers. Get curious about what shapes you. Whatever shows up—even the awkward, messy stuff—that's your curriculum.

I like to visualize limiting beliefs as handcuffs that I've placed on myself. Not knowingly, but now that I see them that way, when I want to set them down, that's what I do. I just take them off and set them down. They aren't locked. I may not have been the one to actually put the cuffs on, but I am the one who keeps them there. I have full authority to throw out anything that doesn't work for me, and so do you. No permission required, no secret code, just set them down. You have the power of choice to do that!

DON'T GET STUCK WITH OLD BELIEFS

A lot of limiting beliefs come from our childhood conditioning. We just feel like that's how we were raised, and that's how it is. It's important to realize that certain things are brought forward from your childhood or other people that maybe don't resonate with you. The limiting belief that you can't just change how you feel, see, or act about something is a powerful one. I highly recommend that you start by throwing that limiting belief out.

You can let go of limiting beliefs if they don't resonate with you. You'd never know that if you weren't willing to look in the mirror and see what truly makes up who you are. When you're brave enough to notice what doesn't land and willing to do the work to toss it out, you create space for so much awesomeness. Then you get to choose what *does* resonate with you. You get to choose what goes into your equation. You don't have to keep playing only the hand you were dealt; you can swap out cards anytime you want.

I toss out limiting beliefs like junk mail, probably because I got handed a lifetime subscription to them as a kid. I grew up in a strict, organized religious household where limiting beliefs were planted and nurtured. Now I stop and call it out: "That's not mine. Why the hell do I think like that?" And just like that, I've been able to rewire a ton of old programming.

There's nothing more powerful than owning your part and refusing to hide behind excuses. Deciding you're not going to keep playing the same tired hand you were dealt; that's real strength. And all it costs is you being willing to get to know yourself.

Once you've decided to own your part, the biggest enemy you'll face is the excuse. And excuses? They're poison. They slime your spirit. Think about the last time you made one. Did it make you feel stronger? Or did it leave you feeling like you let yourself down? Exactly. Stop doing that to yourself. You're worth way more than the cheap cover story an excuse gives you.

Life Hack: Stash a notebook in your car. Stoplights make surprisingly great brainstorming sessions. It beats trolling Instagram or texting someone that you'll be right there. They'll find out when you get there.

CHALLENGE: SILENCE THE NOISE

I challenge you to find a moment of stillness. Step away from the noise, the screens, and the distractions. If possible, go outside, get into nature, even if it's just a park bench or your backyard. Bring a journal. Sit with yourself. No phone. No distraction. Just you.

Start writing, whatever comes to mind. Don't worry about making sense or sounding profound. This isn't about performance; it's about presence. Be curious, not critical. Ask yourself: *How do I actually feel right now?* Not how you think you should feel. Not what someone else expects you to feel. What's true for you, underneath it all?

That's where the magic begins—honest reflection. That's where clarity lives. That's where change takes root.

If your mind goes blank, just write about your day. Start with the basics. As you go, pay attention to moments that felt "off" or emotional. When you hit a spot that feels sticky or charged, pause… and lean in with curiosity. That's a place worth exploring. That's where your growth is waiting.

WARNING—Savage Truth Bomb: not everything is about you. Read that again… *not everything is about you.* Most people are too wrapped in their own lives to be plotting against you. Stop making yourself the center of every storyline; it's ridiculous. In the rare case someone is intentionally trying to poke you, so what? You don't have to suffer because of it. You're the one who chooses to suffer. STOP IT!

CHAPTER 3
FIX YOUR SHIT

One of the most transformative principles I've embraced in my journey is something I now live by: FIX.YOUR.SHIT!

Fix Your Shit! Don't just patch it up for your own sake. Do it so you quit tripping over the same damn cracks in your own sidewalk. Your unhealed mess doesn't stay in your lane… it leaks. It seeps into your relationships, your work, your family, your kids. Every time you dodge dealing with your own baggage, you're handing it off like a toxic relay baton to the next poor soul who crosses your path.

Fixing your shit isn't just about making your life easier—it's about breaking the cycles, cleaning up the wreckage, and refusing to keep repeating the same dumpster-fire patterns. You can't build a life you love on top of rotting foundations. So grab the shovel, dig deep, and handle it. Fix Your Shit! This phrase became a personal mantra as I dove deeper into self-awareness. I realized I was carrying so much—so much unprocessed pain I never let myself feel, so many "rules" I never agreed to, stuck to me like invisible chains, so many emotional landmines disguised as "personality traits." I was dragging around anger, guilt, and fear that had hardened into habits I mistook for *me*. And while some of it wasn't my fault, it was absolutely my responsibility to fix it. Healing it became my work.

As I peeled back the layers, I uncovered wounds that demanded attention. Some only needed acknowledgement, while others had to be torn down, burned to the ground, and rebuilt from scratch. But every single one of them was shaping my daily life, whether I realized it or not. And here's the catch—unhealed wounds don't stay buried. They leak out sideways, showing up as the very thing we casually label as "triggers."

We've turned being "triggered" into a badge of honor. People say things like, "That totally triggered me," or "Ugh, every time he does that, it's such a trigger." But let's cut the bullshit! What you're really saying is, "That hit an unhealed wound I've been running from." Your triggers are not someone else's problem. And mine, sure as hell, aren't yours. What *is* your problem is how you show up when life pokes those raw spots. Are you going to blow up, play the victim, and torch your day, your relationships, your opportunities? Or are you finally going to get brutally curious and deal with your own mess?

Stop steamrolling the people in your life because they forgot your favorite color, said a word you put on your personal no-fly list, or didn't memorize all 47 of your emotional tripwires. That's not trauma-informed... that's tyrannical. Expecting everyone to tiptoe around your unhealed wounds is like handing out a manual titled *How to Keep Me Comfortable at All Costs* and then getting pissed when no one follows it. Newsflash: The world isn't your emotional babysitter.

I don't know who started the trend of "avoiding triggers," but congratulations... you've invented the fastest way to stay stuck. Triggers aren't landmines to sidestep; they're neon billboards screaming *"FIX THIS SHIT."* Dodging them is like ignoring the check engine light on your car and then acting shocked when the engine blows. You don't heal by bubble-wrapping yourself from discomfort. You heal by walking straight into the fire and dealing with it.

Triggers are our teachers. A trigger is an invitation to examine something beneath the surface. It's a flare from your subconscious saying: *Hey, there's a wound here that needs your attention.* Consider it a homework assignment in the University of Life.

When something triggers you, before you do anything else, pause, and ask yourself:

1. *Why did that affect me the way it did?*
2. *Is this really about what just happened, or is it something resurfacing from the past?*
3. *Is this belief helping me or holding me back?*

Without that questioning, we end up dragging our emotional baggage around, expecting others to handle it like it's explosive. We want people to walk carefully so they don't set off our emotional landmines. But that's not healing and living fully. That's just surviving. Stop giving away the power of your peace to other people.

You're not broken—you were wired for survival. But survival mode isn't your best life. Quit bleeding on people who didn't cut you. Quit handing out your baggage like it's a party favor. Own it. Heal it. FIX YOUR SHIT!

YOU'RE NOT CRAZY, YOU'VE BEEN CONDITIONED

Many of us were shaped by things we never asked for. Some were raised in homes with addiction, abuse, or neglect. Others never felt emotionally safe. Some learned early on that love was conditional, that safety wasn't guaranteed, or that vulnerability wasn't safe.

These experiences hardwire our nervous systems. They make us guarded. Defensive. Hypervigilant. And then we carry all that into adulthood, applying survival-mode thinking to everyday situations that don't actually threaten us. A text message left on *"read"* becomes rejection. An innocent question becomes a personal attack. Silence becomes abandonment. You're not crazy. You're just continuing to react to old pain. But you don't have to live like that.

One of the best resources I've ever found for breaking out of those old patterns is *The Four Agreements* by Don Miguel Ruiz. It's simple, powerful, and cuts right to the heart of how we relate to ourselves and others. The agreements—be impeccable with your word, don't take anything personally, don't make assumptions, and always do your best—are basically a blueprint for dismantling survival-mode thinking. Friendly warning: Skip the fluffy intro and outro unless you're really into that flavor of woo-woo. The real magic is in the core chapters... the meat and potatoes. That's where the work lives, and it lines up perfectly with what we're talking about here.

Stop building emotional scaffolding. When we experience pain, we often build mental scaffolding around it for protection. Something hurts us, and instead of letting it go, we wrap it in rules, beliefs, and defense mechanisms to prevent it from happening or hurting us again. We do this to avoid feeling that pain again. The problem is: Now we've built an elaborate prison.

All that scaffolding makes vulnerability difficult. It makes true intimacy nearly impossible. We don't want anyone to get close enough to hurt us, so we keep everyone at a distance, even the people that love us most. But real connection lives on the other side of that vulnerability. And to get there, you have to be willing to dismantle the scaffolding and look at what's underneath.

THE POWER OF THE BUFFALO

There's a parable I love, and it's one I come back to often.

Out on the Great Plains, when a storm is coming, the cattle instinctively run away from it. They try to outrun the thunder, the lightning, the pain. But they can't. In running from the storm, they end up stuck beneath it longer—moving with it instead of through it.

But buffalo? Buffalo do the opposite. When they see a storm on the horizon, they charge into it. They run into the chaos. Into the discomfort. Into the unknown. They don't avoid the pain. They face it. And because they do, they move through the storm more quickly. They reach clearer skies, cleaner air, and drier ground faster than the animals who tried to run.

That's the work. That's the model. Be the buffalo!

Don't numb out. Don't retreat. Don't distract yourself with Netflix, food, sex, alcohol, drugs, shopping, or pretending everything is fine. Lean in. Face the discomfort. Go through the storm. Because avoiding the pain doesn't make it go away; it just ensures you stay stuck inside it longer.

Here's something that knocked me on my ass once I finally saw it clearly: Most of the time, we are the source of our own suffering. It's not actually about what someone else said or did. It's about how we reacted, the story we told ourselves, or the way we took it personally. We create our own private hells, brick by brick, and then wonder why life feels so overwhelming.

Think about it. Someone makes a comment, and instead of letting it roll off, we attach meaning to it. We explode, shut down, spiral, or stew in silence, and then blame the world for the chaos we created. We hand out front-row seats to our drama and act surprised when the show is a disaster.

But what if, in those moments, you hit pause instead of detonate? What if you counted to ten, took a deep breath, or even asked yourself one simple question: *What's really going on here?* That tiny moment of curiosity can change everything. Instead of reacting out of old wounds, you're choosing to respond from a place of awareness. And awareness is the first step out of the prison you built for yourself.

Try these next time you get triggered:

- Flex curiosity instead of snapping back.
- Throw down reflection instead of getting defensive.
- Lead with compassion instead of playing judge and jury.

These are the tools of someone who is fixing their shit. And they are learned, practiced, earned. The second you start fixing your shit, everything changes. Life opens doors you didn't even know existed, and the ripple effects will blow you away.

My life today is beyond anything I could have imagined for myself. And I don't think that's luck or coincidence. I know it's because I fixed and continue to fix my shit and I am committed to the concepts I'm sharing in this book. Every time I did the work, peeled back another layer, and faced what I'd been avoiding, life expanded. The more I leaned in, the bigger the payoff. That's not theory; that's lived proof.

Healing is yours to do, no one else's. Childhood scars? Toxic exes? Life's hard knocks? Maybe not your fault. Doesn't matter. What matters is this: healing is your responsibility.

Waiting for someone else to fix it won't work. Waiting for time to do it won't work. Ignoring it definitely won't work. **You** have to do the work. Because if you don't, you'll keep living the same patterns, reacting the same way, sabotaging the same opportunities, and hurting the same people over and over. And eventually, you'll start to believe that life just is this way. But it's not. You're just running away from the storm.

Doing the work is not easy. I won't lie to you. It's painful. It's humbling. It requires you to face the ugliest parts of your story and sit with things you wish you could forget.

But what's on the other side of the work? Freedom. Peace. Self-trust. Connection. And most of all… clarity.

We all want to be loved. We all want to feel safe. We all want to live fully. You can't do that if your past is still running the show. You can't do that while you're dragging emotional wreckage like a ball and chain. You can't do that if every one of your relationships is shaped by wounds someone else gave you.

But you can choose differently. You can be brave. You can be the buffalo. Run into the storm. Face it. Feel it. Fix it! Because clear skies are waiting on the other side.

CHALLENGE: THE TRIGGER TAKEDOWN

Take a step towards fixing your shit:

1. Get quiet. Step away from the noise.
2. Grab a journal. Be honest with yourself.
3. Ask yourself, *What am I dragging around that no longer serves me?*
4. Name a trigger. Write: "I have a trigger around [insert situation]."
5. Ask. What belief is tied to this? Is it true? Is it useful?
6. Get curious. Not judgmental. Curious.

You're not here to live a half-life bound by your past. You're here to live free. But that starts with fixing your shit!

CHAPTER 4
EQ = EMOTIONAL INTELLIGENCE

Emotional intelligence (EQ... like IQ, but with an E for emotional) is the ability to understand, manage, and express your emotions while also recognizing and responding to the emotions of others. In simple terms: It's knowing how to use your feelings as data, a built-in navigation system for life. And when you get it right? It's powerful.

In recent years, I've become obsessed with emotions and emotional intelligence. Most people I ask can't even define EQ, let alone describe how it shows up in their lives. Fascinating—and sad. Because just by learning to notice and use my emotions, I've gained more knowledge about myself and the world than I ever thought possible. Managing my feelings, reading others', and navigating life with that awareness? Honestly, it's turned into a game. And it's the best game I've ever played.

I spent the first forty years of my life completely emotionally illiterate. I believed with my whole chest that showing feelings was weakness, that vulnerability meant you didn't have it all together. Damn, was I wrong. And when my body *did* start feeling things, I stuffed them down and slapped a lid on tight, like shaking up a soda can and pretending it wouldn't eventually explode. Obviously, it did... enter Rehab 2016.

Today, emotional intelligence and vulnerability are my superpowers. I feel like Wonder Woman. Had I known life could feel this good, I would've sprinted to rock bottom decades earlier. Of course, that's not how it works. Life has its own timeline. Still, it's wild to imagine how different my twenties and thirties might have been if I'd had this wisdom back then. But I'm not here to play the woulda, coulda, shoulda game. I'm here, in my forties, doing the work. Better late than never.

But it can't stop with me finally figuring it out in my forties. Waiting until adulthood is like learning to swim after you've already been tossed in the deep end: frantic, exhausting, and way harder than it has to be. Imagine if kids grew up fluent in their own feelings instead of having to untangle the mess later in life. I've seen the shift in my own family. Before we made this transition, my kids reacted the way most of us were taught: stuff it down, explode, or slap on a fake smile. "Suck it up." "Don't cry." "Be strong." That's the emotional inheritance we'd been passing down for generations. But now, instead of defaulting to shutdown or blow-up, they pause, name what they're feeling, and work through it. It's not perfect... but it's healthy. And it's proof that when you change the pattern, the ripple effect hits the next generation immediately.

We raise kids to perform under emotional pressure but never give them the playbook to handle it. We expect kids to perform in school, in friendships, in sports, in life, but we don't give them the tools to understand or manage the feelings that fuel all of it. That's not just unfair; it's like setting them up to drown before they even get a chance to swim.

Emotions aren't optional; they're essential.

When we fail to give kids tools to understand and manage their feelings, we set them up to struggle. Emotional intelligence shouldn't be reserved for therapy sessions or self-help books; it belongs in everyday conversations, especially with children. For too long we've denied both kids and adults the compass they need. Emotions are that compass. They guide our choices, shape our relationships, and steer us through challenges. It's time to stop shortchanging the next generation.

For me, growing up, emotions looked messy, chaotic, and overwhelming. I wanted nothing to do with them. I stuffed them down, pushed them away, and prided myself on being the tomboy who stayed "in control." Men didn't seem to deal with emotions, so that became my playbook. Let's get it straight: emotions aren't weakness; they're intel. Once I stopped ignoring them, I realized they were handing me the damn instruction manual. And now that I have the map, I'm savage about chasing truth and stacking knowledge.

Blowing off emotional intelligence is like tossing your GPS out the window and then bragging about "finding your own way." Sure, you'll get somewhere eventually, but expect wrong turns, burnout, and crash-and-burn moments. Control isn't the problem—the illusion of control is. You think you're steering the wheel, but you're just gripping it tighter while life drives anyway. You don't have it; you never did. If you're a control freak—been there, done that—you're just white-knuckling through life with a false sense of power. There's a better way, but first you have to unclench.

How can you benefit from emotions if you don't even recognize them? Think about how so many boys were told, "Don't be a pussy. Man up. Stop crying, or I'll give you something to cry about." We taught boys that processing emotions was weakness, and now we wonder why so many men are angry, detached, or numb. What a massive disservice. Our sons, husbands, brothers, and fathers deserve better. Collectively, we have to fix this belief. Because when we shut emotions down, generation after generation, we handicap ourselves.

People suffer because they suck at handling their emotions. They've shelved their greatest tool and let it collect dust. This isn't judgment; it's truth. Get curious. Learn. Upgrade. If emotional intelligence isn't your strong suit yet, no shame, but no excuses either. Your life gets exponentially better the moment you stop running from your emotions and start mastering them.

Ask yourself: *What's my relationship with my emotions: friend, enemy, or total stranger?* If nobody gave you the tools to deal with your feelings, that's not your fault. But ignoring them now? That's on you. There's no shame in starting late, only power in finally showing up.

When you're ready to tackle this, come at it with raw curiosity and zero filters. What's the risk in telling yourself the truth? In the beginning, don't try to change anything. Just notice. Pay attention without judgment. That practice alone can change everything.

When something happens, pause and ask: *How does this make me feel? What's this emotion trying to tell me?* Your feelings aren't random; they're messages. They're guides. That's their purpose. We're all here to work through our stuff, learn from it, and use it to level up.

Life itself is a classroom. A lifelong university. The curriculum is learning about yourself, the people you've chosen to do life with, and the world around you. When you're open to growth, when you compete only with yesterday's version of yourself, you break free of the rinse-and-repeat hamster wheel. You tap into a deeper purpose.

Doing this work is fascinating, but more than that, it's the most important work you'll ever do. It shapes you into the best possible version of yourself, for your sake and for everyone around you. And remember, this isn't about criticism; it's about curiosity. Notice. Journal. Reflect. Get curious and watch what unfolds.

Triggers are gold mines. If a friend says something that stings, don't react. Count to ten. Pause. Ask yourself, *Why did that land so hard?* I promise, it's not about them. It's about unresolved stuff inside you. That's your work. When you notice and unpack those moments, you stop letting triggers run the show. Emotions stop being wrecking balls and start becoming compasses. They'll point you toward the exact places you need to heal, if you're willing to pay attention.

When you ignore emotions instead of working with them, they become a tangled mess of frustration and resentment. On the outside, you might look fine, even happy. But underneath is the weight of not living your truth. And that weight builds quietly until one day it's too heavy to carry. That's the cost of avoidance.

So we numb ourselves. Food. Alcohol. Shopping. TV. Porn. Doom scrolling. You can numb with almost anything. I take no exception with intentional numbing. We all need a breather. But mindless numbing? That's where it gets dangerous. That's when you become a zombie in your own story.

MASTER YOUR EMOTIONS, MASTER THE GAME

Once you learn to use your emotions as a tool, nobody can take that from you. You gain the ability to navigate a more joyful, productive, and peaceful life. Nothing external changes, just your understanding of yourself and how you engage with the world. That shift alone can improve your life times ten.

There's no secret recipe. It really is this simple: Get curious about yourself. Learn your emotions. Use them. Brené Brown's *Atlas of the Heart* is a great resource; it maps out the wide spectrum of feelings, how to name them, and why language matters. When you can identify your emotions, you gain clarity, meaning, and choice. Without that, you're just reacting.

My recommendation: Start small. Get curious about one moment a day. What happened? What did you feel? How could you respond differently next time? Practice the ten-second rule: When triggered, pause before reacting. That small pause creates room for awareness, reflection, and emotional intelligence to take the wheel.

Over time, it gets easier. Each pause, each moment of curiosity, builds your skill set. It's like leveling up in a video game: master one trigger, move on to the next. Before long, you'll see patterns you never noticed and experience freedom you didn't think was possible.

Life isn't random. Lessons repeat until you learn them. If the same thing keeps happening, that's the universe nudging you. Get curious, respond differently, pass the level, and move forward. That's how you grow. That's how you fix your shit.

Practicing mindfulness to become aware of automatic reactions is also an excellent way to take back control of your life. What are you doing without even thinking about it because you're not aware? We get sucked into negative patterns that drag us down, and half the time we don't even realize we're doing it.

How many of your daily habits are on autopilot? These aren't conscious choices; they're default settings that creep in when you're not paying attention. Here are a few ways those automatic reactions sneak into everyday life:

- Snapping at your kids or partner after a stressful day—not because of them, but because of what you're carrying.

- Grabbing your phone before your feet hit the floor in the morning and diving into other people's lives before your own.
- Pouring a drink at night, not because you want it, but because it's the routine.
- Scrolling mindlessly on social media, then wondering why you feel worse afterward.
- Saying yes when your whole body is screaming no.
- Eating until you're stuffed because you weren't tuned in to your hunger.
- Ignoring your gut reaction, only to realize later you were right all along.
- Driving to work on autopilot and barely remembering the trip once you get there.

Mindfulness is the switch you flip when you finally say, "I want better. I want to live my best life, because nothing is guaranteed—not even tomorrow."

Guess what: It's not just your thoughts you need to catch. Your body has been screaming at you, too.

GUT CHECK

So many of us feel like our gut doesn't work anymore. We say things like, *"I just can't trust my instincts,"* or *"My radar must be broken."* Fact: Your gut was never broken. You've just been self-betraying for so long that your body is clogged up with static. Every time you said yes when you wanted to scream no, every time you swallowed your truth to keep the peace, every time you ignored that tight knot in your stomach because you didn't want to deal with the fallout, you trained yourself to override your own internal compass.

Your gut is like a compass that's been shoved in a junk drawer. It still points north. It just needs you to clear off all of the crap it's buried under. Rebuilding trust in yourself is the work. It means listening when your body whispers instead of waiting for it to scream. It means noticing when your stomach clenches, your chest tightens, or your skin prickles, and treating those signals like the high-priority alerts they are.

Your gut is not optional. It's your most primal, finely tuned survival system. Ignore it, and you drift. Honor it, and you navigate.

You can't outsource your instincts. No guru, no checklist, no life hack can replace the wisdom wired into your body. If you want to stop drifting and start actually steering your life, you've got to stop betraying yourself and start rebuilding that gut-level trust.

Your mind can spin stories. Your heart can get tangled up in feelings. But your gut? Your gut is pure truth. And when you finally start listening to it again, you'll find yourself standing on solid ground you didn't even know was there.

So flip the switch. Tune in. And remember, ignoring your gut has been costing you. Trusting it will change everything.

GUT REHAB: SAVAGE EDITION

If your gut feels gunked up from years of self-betrayal, here are three quick ways to start scraping off the muck and rebuilding trust with yourself:

1. **Track the Twinge.** Notice every time your stomach knots, your chest tightens, or you feel that "something's off" buzz. Don't judge it, don't fix it, just write it down. (This is your gut whispering. You've been ignoring it for years. Time to listen.)

2. **Reverse the Yes.** When you feel yourself about to say yes but your body is screaming no, pause. Say no. Even if it's awkward. Even if people look at you sideways. That single choice is like doing a hard reset on your inner compass.
3. **Micro-Trust Reps.** Start small: Do I want to say yes to this invite, or would I rather eat tacos in sweatpants? Do I bite my tongue, or finally say the thing out loud? Do I keep doomscrolling, or shut it down and go live my own damn life? Ask, then follow the first nudge you feel. It's like gym class for your intuition. The reps add up.

The reality is, your gut doesn't lie. It never has. You just stopped listening. Time to get quiet, tune in, and give yourself permission to follow it again.

CHALLENGE: EQ IN ACTION

Think of a recent conflict with a friend, family member, or coworker. How did you respond? Did you overreact? Did you shut down? Did you give yourself space to process? Write it down, then replay the situation in two ways: First as you handled it, and then as the emotionally intelligent version of you would handle it. Compare the outcomes. That awareness alone can shift everything.

Note: This work is *the* work. The better you get at emotional intelligence, the better your life gets, period. Don't numb out. Don't white-knuckle it. Get curious. Notice. Learn. Your emotions are your compass. Follow them, and they'll take you exactly where you need to go.

CHAPTER 5
PERSPECTIVE

Have you ever seen the image of two people standing on opposite sides of a number? One swears it's a 6, the other swears it's a 9. Both are digging in their heels, convinced they're right and the other one is a total idiot. Come to find out, they're both right. Welcome to the mess we call "perspective."

Life is basically one giant 6/9 fight. Your boss calls you lazy; you call it refusing to bleed out for a broken system. Your partner calls it nagging; you call it being sick of carrying their dead weight. Your mom calls it attitude; you call it finally drawing the line. Your friend calls it selfish; you call it protecting your peace. And in traffic? Someone cuts you off and they're Satan's cousin. You cut someone off, and it's, "Chill, Karen, I just need to merge." Perspective is everything.

Reality isn't what happens. Reality is the story you tell yourself about what happens. And most of us suck at telling that story. We grab the worst angle, the ugliest version, and then cling to it like gospel. That's like looking at a 6 and refusing to turn your head to see the damn 9.

This may be hard for some of you to read: Your perspective isn't fact. It's just an angle. Shift the angle, and the whole damn thing changes.

Think of perspective like a disco ball. Every one of us is a tiny, mirrored tile, reflecting light from a slightly different angle. No two people get the exact same view... not even if they're standing shoulder to shoulder. Why? Because they're still looking through their own filters: their history, their scars, their gender, their race, their culture, their beliefs, their mood that day. Your perspective isn't *the* truth; it's just one sliver of the light show. The more you can step back and notice all those reflections bouncing around, the easier it is to understand that reality is a whole lot bigger than your little square of glass. And when you realize that? You stop fighting over who's right and start enjoying the damn dance floor.

That's the power of perspective. It's not about proving your square is shinier than someone else's. It's about recognizing the whole ball spins brighter when all the angles show up. Shift your view, and suddenly what felt like conflict turns into connection. When you insist your perspective is the only one that matters, it's like duct-taping a disco ball so only your tile shows. Not only do you kill the light show, but you also look ridiculous standing in the dark with your roll of tape.

Perspective isn't just about how you see other people. It's also about how you see your own problems. The lens you use can either magnify the chaos or reveal the calm.

I was working with someone recently who was completely overwhelmed. They were rattling off this laundry list of things they needed to work through: work drama, family stress, personal baggage... the whole nine yards. I could see it on their face: They were drowning in "too much."

So I gave them an example they weren't expecting. I asked if they knew what a metronome was. You know, that little triangle thing that sits on top of a piano and swings back and forth to keep time. At the very top of the pendulum bar, when it swings, it looks like it's covering so much distance from one side to the other. It feels like it's forever away from balance. But if you shift your perspective and look at it from the bottom, near the pivot point, the swing barely moves at all. It's a tiny shift. Same swing, totally different experience depending on where you're looking.

That's life. At the "top," when we're caught in overwhelm, every task feels huge. Every obligation looks like miles to cross. But if you change your vantage point, even slightly, you realize the distance isn't that big. It's literally that simple. The shifted perspective collapses the gap.

Another important way to look at perspective: You get to shift from *"I have to"* into *"I get to."* That's not just semantics; it's a reframe that will change everything. "I have to do laundry" becomes "I get to have clean clothes." "I have to go to work" becomes "I get to earn money and provide for my family." "I have to pick up my kids" becomes "I get to spend time with them while they're still small enough to think I'm cool."

Sure, at first it feels a little ridiculous, like you're trying to trick yourself. That's just your brain realizing it's under new management. Keep practicing it. Keep flipping "have to" into "get to," and watch how your outlook transforms. Suddenly, chores aren't chores. Obligations aren't chains. They become opportunities.

Pro Tip: Implement this daily. Every time "I have to" comes up, flip it into "I get to." Say it out loud if you need to. Your stress goes down, your gratitude goes up, and your fulfillment skyrockets.

Don't mistake this little life hack for a free pass to tolerate garbage. If you're in situations that are out of alignment with your peace and your purpose—relationships, jobs, environments that drain you—it's not about sugarcoating them with a "get to" and pretending they're fine. If it needs an overhaul, then overhaul it. Rip off the band-aid. Burn the bridge. Redesign the damn thing.

But for the stuff that's simply part of being human—laundry, traffic, bills, cleaning up the kitchen after your kids wreck it—don't let your brain screw you out of your own joy by turning them into anchors. Those things are neutral until your perspective paints them as suffering. You can either drag yourself through them kicking and bitching the whole way, or you can flip the script and lighten your own load.

That's the difference: Overhaul what's broken. Reframe what's necessary. Both give you back energy. Both put you back in charge.

The story that really drove this lesson home for me wasn't about laundry or errands. It was about my daughter. She's faced more challenges than most people will ever see in a lifetime. There was a season when she was calling me constantly, and my son would often be in the car when the phone rang. Every time, he'd sigh and ask, "Do you have to answer that?"

And my response was always the same: "No, bud. I don't have to. I get to."

Vulnerability talking: There was a long stretch of time, longer than I want to admit, when we weren't sure our daughter was going to make it. It was hospital stays, suicide attempts, rehabs, and so much darkness. During those years, I lived in fear of the phone ringing and it being the *wrong* kind of call... the one no parent wants to get.

So now? That love muffin could call me a thousand times a day, and I will *always* get to answer. It's never a "have to." It's a privilege. A reminder that she's still here, still fighting, still reaching out.

That's the heart of this whole mindset shift. "I get to" isn't about blind positivity. It's about remembering that even the hard, messy parts of life can hold gratitude if you zoom out and change the angle.

Transforming an obligation into something you *get* to do changes everything. It's gratitude in action. You're no longer just slogging through life; you're choosing how to show up for it. And that choice? That's massive. Most people don't even realize they *have* it. They live like life is happening *to* them, like they're stuck in a riptide, just waiting for the next wave to knock them flat.

EVERY CHOICE SHAPES YOUR LIFE

Life isn't happening to you. You're happening to it. You're not some powerless bystander. You're the one steering! And if you keep getting knocked over by the same damn waves, maybe it's time to stop standing there and try something different.

You always have a choice. How you respond. How you engage. How much energy you give away or protect. Every choice carries energy. Every choice tilts the scale. When you make them mindlessly, you end up drained, resentful, and stuck. When you make them with intention, you take the wheel back. You shape your experience instead of letting it shape you.

And here's the part most people miss: Doing nothing is still a choice. Pretending you're powerless doesn't get you off the hook. It just keeps you in the same place. But when you shift even one small "have to" into a "get to," that single reframe alters your entire relationship with it. Work stops feeling like punishment and starts feeling like opportunity. Relationships stop being drains and start being investments. Growth stops being a burden and starts being a privilege.

There will always be things you can't change: curveballs, chaos, circumstances outside your control. But how you respond to them? That's always on you. How you process them, how you carry them, how you let them shape the next step in your life...

those are your decisions. And that kind of ownership? That's not just power. That's freedom.

Living from a place rooted in gratitude will change your life. Full stop. You get to decide where your energy goes. That's the power of your choice. When you deliberately focus on what you already have and what's going right instead of obsessing about what's missing, you shift your whole vibration. That single shift creates space for more good things to flow in.

Energy is contagious. The vibe you put out is the vibe you get back. If you're constantly negative, always criticizing, always pointing out what's wrong, you're basically sending an engraved invitation for more of that crap to land on your doorstep. And people who live in gratitude? They're not sticking around for your pity party. Positive people avoid constant complainers the same way you'd avoid stepping in dog shit. It doesn't match the energy they're trying to keep.

At some point, everyone makes a choice, whether consciously or not, to live positively or negatively. You decide the lens you're going to see life through. So, if you're wading through life looking for what's broken, unfair, or disappointing, guess what? That's exactly what you'll find and what you're inviting into your house every single day. On the flip side, when you choose happiness, even when circumstances suck, you shift your power. The world might be crumbling, but you can still laugh, still smile, still dance in the wreckage. Will people think you're crazy? Probably. Does it matter? Not even a little. You decide whether you're going to be a positive or negative force. It really is that simple.

If you can't find something positive to say, shut your mouth. Positive people look for solutions. Negative people look for excuses. Your spirit hears you either way. Every negative word, every excuse, every complaint—your body and soul absorb that energy like poison. Words carry power. Thoughts shape reality.

The more aware you are of that truth, the more intentionally you can work *with* your energy instead of against it.

When you live from a negative place, you set yourself up for failure before you even start. Look around at the people who seem happiest and most fulfilled, not the richest or flashiest, but the ones with real peace. Nine times out of ten, they're the ones who choose positivity on purpose. Get curious about that. Who in your life radiates peace? Who seems grounded no matter what? Ask them what they do. Steal their hacks. Put your own spin on it. Success leaves clues... grab them.

Think of negativity and positivity like little batteries. Every battery has two sides: a + side and a − side. When you're "+ side up," you naturally attract other + batteries. You'll find yourself drawn to people, opportunities, and energy that match that charge. On the flip side (literally), when you're "− side up," you'll start sticking to other negative batteries. Misery loves company because that's how energy works. It's magnets in motion.

You always have the ability to flip your battery. Picture a little watch battery or one of those tiny, round disc batteries. You don't need a degree in electrical engineering. You don't need to rewire your whole system. All you have to do is flip the damn thing over. That's perspective.

Are you facing the world with your + side or your − side showing? If you don't like what you're attracting, maybe it's time to stop blaming everyone else and flip your own battery.

And here's where we circle back: gratitude practice. I can't hammer this home enough. It's not just "nice." It's not optional. Gratitude is the foundation of perspective. If you want to rewire your brain, start a gratitude journal. It takes minutes a day. Write ten things. Start a note in your phone called "Good Things Are Always Happening to Me." Set reminders if you need to. Keep the journal where you'll actually use it. At first, it might feel awkward or forced to list ten things. But the more you practice, the more you realize how much you already have... and that shift? Total game changer. If one version doesn't click, adjust and try again until something does. The point isn't perfection... it's traction. Leave a notebook by your bed, write it on a bar napkin, or scrawl it on the back of a Target receipt. Nobody cares how—just quit making excuses and put the damn words down.

Journaling is the single most effective way I've found to shift perspective. When you write, you process. When you process, you see differently. And when you see differently, you live differently. That's the ripple effect of gratitude. It turns burdens into blessings, "have to" into "get to," and it flips your 6 into a 9. That's the power of perspective.

Your gratitude practice doesn't have to be complicated. Sometimes my daily list includes things that are tiny, like my coffee being exactly the right temperature. Sometimes they're huge, like a breakthrough conversation with someone I love.

When you come with gratitude instead of scarcity or fear, your entire vibration changes. Everything is about perspective, and gratitude is the fastest way to shift yours. Gratitude reframes the way you see your world. You start scanning for positives instead of negatives. Practice gratitude first thing in the morning, or right before bed. Either way, the thought becomes: *What am I going to notice today so I've got something to write down later?*

I could sit down right now and rattle off a list of everything I don't have. And let's be real, I'd never run out of material. I could keep that list going straight through to my last breath. There's always more you *don't* have: more money, more status, more stuff, more whatever-the-hell you think you're missing. If that's the game you want to play, have at it. You'll never "lose," because lack is infinite. You'll always find another gap, another comparison, another way to convince yourself you're behind.

Focusing on what's missing is like drinking poison and then wondering why you feel sick. You *can* make that your identity... someone who constantly measures life by what isn't there. Plenty of people do. And guess what? They stay stuck, bitter, and exhausted.

The shift comes when you flip the script. Instead of obsessing over what you don't have, you start getting intentional about what you *do* have. Gratitude isn't fluffy bullshit. It's a perspective shift that rewires your brain. When you look at your life through the lens of abundance instead of lack, your entire experience changes. The traffic jam becomes extra time to finish a podcast. The slow cashier becomes a reminder to slow your own roll. The tiny apartment becomes the cozy place you get to call home.

This doesn't mean you stop striving. It means you stop suffering while you strive. Gratitude doesn't erase ambition. It fuels it. Because when you're not drained by scarcity, you've actually got the energy to go after more.

So yeah, you could keep making that endless list of everything missing from your life. Or you could flip the 6 into a 9, start counting what you already have, and watch your enjoyment of life skyrocket. It's not magic. It's perspective. And it will blow your mind how fast it changes everything.

CHALLENGE: BORROWED LENSES

Pick one person in your life who you believe has the best chance of being non-judgmental with you. Not the person who always tries to "fix" you. Not the one who gossips. The one who can actually hold space.

Then lead with vulnerability. Share something you're struggling with: a fear, a frustration, a story from your past or present that feels heavy. Don't dress it up. Don't sugarcoat it. Just be real.

Once you've put it on the table, ask them one simple question: "What's your perspective?"

The goal isn't for them to hand you all the answers; it's to let you see the situation through someone else's lens. Sometimes that fresh angle is exactly what you need to break the loop in your own head.

Remember: Perspective is everything. If life looks like a 6 to you right now, their input might just help you see the 9.

CHAPTER 6
MENTAL STRENGTH: STOP IT

Your mind is a powerhouse, but left unchecked, it's also a total drama queen. It'll drag you through endless replays of awkward conversations, spiral into "what ifs," and blow molehills into mountains. That same intensity can fuel clarity, confidence, and joy when you learn to point it in the right direction. The power doesn't disappear. It just needs to be trained. Your mind isn't meant to be silenced; it's meant to be steered.

Building mental strength isn't easy, but it's a total power move. At first, it feels awkward, like trying to lift weights with spaghetti arms. Especially if you've let your inner critic run wild for years. I hear it all the time, especially from women: "I'm not good enough... I'm not qualified... why even try? It'll never work out." That broken record is exhausting... and wrong. Just because your mind says it doesn't mean it deserves a microphone.

You are not your mind. Your mind is a tool, like your body or your emotions. It's there to serve you, not define you. The thoughts racing through your head? They're just background noise until you choose to act on them. So, if your mind tends to lean negative or hypercritical, that doesn't mean it's "who you are." It just means your tool needs some retraining. And you're the one holding the damn toolbox.

We've let our minds run feral, kind of like my childhood, pure chaos. Social media doesn't help. Five minutes of scrolling and suddenly you're knee-deep in comparison, convinced you're behind in life because everyone else apparently has six-pack abs, a perfect marriage, a side hustle making millions, and toddlers who eat kale chips without crying. Meanwhile, you're sitting there in yesterday's sweatpants, eating cold pizza, wondering if Target still sells happiness in bulk. That spiral right there? That's your inner critic hopped up on caffeine. Left unchecked, it wrecks your peace and hijacks your confidence. But once you realize that voice is just a misused tool, not the truth, you get your power back. The second you grab the reins and redirect it, the game changes.

MEET YOUR PSYCHO ROOMMATE

In *The Untethered Soul*, Michael Singer nails the idea that you are not your mind in such a beautiful way that I can't recommend it enough. That book cracked something open for me. One of the most helpful practices he teaches is to externalize your inner voice, literally imagine it as someone sitting on the couch with you. Now picture this: How long would you hang out with a "friend" who constantly told you you're not good enough, not qualified, or doomed to fail? How long would you let someone trash-talk your kids, your partner, or your best friend the way your mind trashes you? Exactly. You'd toss them out on their ass. Yet, for some reason, we let that voice stay rent-free in our heads, running wild like it owns the place. STOP IT. That voice isn't you; it's a tool gone rogue. And when you finally take the damn wheel, your life changes. Don't let your brain run you. You run it.

Now, I know this might sound too simple... like, *Sure, I'll just stop listening to the psycho roommate in my head. Easy-peasy.* But the truth is, it really can be that simple once you stop feeding the tug-of-war. It takes practice, momentum, and a little bit of humor to get there. My best friend and I decided to make it fun. We named our inner critic. Meet Darla. Darla is a bitch. She's nasty, she's petty, and she has nothing valuable to say.

And here's where I want you to take it further: Give your Darla a face. Borrow my version if she resonates with you. Print her out, curlers and all. Or find a picture, a meme, or whatever visual makes you laugh at your own inner critic. Then post her everywhere you need a reminder that you are not Darla. She's just an unwelcome tenant who needs eviction. Put her on your bathroom mirror, your fridge, your car dashboard, your desk at work. Use her as a bookmark in the book you're reading. Hell, wallpaper your life with Darla until you start getting traction. Because change doesn't happen from reading a clever line in a book. It happens when you set yourself up for success with constant reminders that stick.

Darla's quick with her insults. She's the one whispering that I don't deserve good things, that I'm not worthy, that my thighs are too big, that I'm... fill in the blank with whatever cruel nonsense she's serving up that day. Darla doesn't actually know shit. She's loud, but her track record is garbage. She's about as accurate as a meteorologist. Time and again, Darla says I can't do something, and then I do it... and guess what? Turns out I was good enough the whole damn time. So why am I giving her the microphone like she's an expert?

And yet, we all do it. We let Darla stomp around in our heads like she's the CEO of Truth, handing down verdicts about our worth and our future. It's outrageous. In my mind, she even looks the part, except instead of a sharp suit and corner office, my Darla shows up with curlers still in her hair, giant sunglasses indoors, a cigarette dangling from her lips, a cheap beer clutched in one hand, parked on the toilet like it's her throne. That's who we've promoted to CEO? A train wreck with her underwear around her knees? Would you honestly take life advice from that? Hell no. Yet that's who we let run the show inside our heads. Darla struts in with all the confidence in the world and zero credibility, and we act like she's Oprah. Once you can see your Darla for what she is, a clown, not a coach, you can finally tell her to shut up, sit down, and watch you prove her wrong. That's where your mental muscle starts to flex.

When I got home from rehab, my mind was a full-blown riot. It ran wild, replaying every bad decision, every wreckage I'd left behind. Rehab may have helped me stop drinking, but it didn't come with an instruction manual for how to deal with the noise in my head, or how to handle emotions I'd spent my entire life avoiding.

Up until then, I didn't know how to process emotions at all. My strategy was simple: shove them down, slap on a smile, and pretend I was fine. Over and over again, I stuffed them deep until they had nowhere else to go. But then the granddaddy of emotions showed up on my doorstep... grief. The really nasty kind that blasts a hole in your life.

My sister's death wrecked me. I didn't know how to function. On the outside, I went through the motions of life. On the inside, I was drowning. I numbed myself with alcohol (more so than I already had been), made bad choices, and blamed myself in twisted ways that made no sense. I couldn't save her, and somehow my brain turned that into "your fault." Grief had me by the throat, and instead of facing it, I ran... from the pain, from myself, from everything that mattered. Those two years were a slow-motion demolition of my life.

A few months after rehab, I was back at my vanity, lost in the chaos of my own mind. My thoughts were relentless, an endless loop of destruction I couldn't shut down. I tried to interrupt the patterns, to redirect, to change the channel. And maybe for a second, it worked. But two seconds later, the spiral came roaring back. That's when it hit me: This was going to be one of the hardest things I'd ever do, but it was non-negotiable. If I wanted a better life, I had to take my mind back. Because when your mind isn't right, it's like having the threat inside your own house. You're under attack, not from the world, but from yourself.

As I sat there at my vanity, drowning in mental noise, I decided to do one simple thing: Light a candle. That tiny act was enough to break the cycle, to shift my attention away from the destructive thought loop I was spiraling into. Suddenly, instead of being pummeled by my own mind, I had something tangible to focus on. The flame was steady. The flame was real. And for a few minutes, I wasn't lost in the chaos of my head. That's what I was trying to do... interrupt the hamster wheel. Because that's exactly what it felt like: Darla running in circles, shrieking nonsense, beating me up with thoughts that weren't helping anyone.

So, I started using candles as my reset button. Any time Darla kicked up her noise, I'd strike a match. Sometimes I'd have candles burning all over my house, like my own personal lighthouse system, each flame pulling me back to the present, away from the chaos. At first, I wasn't replacing Darla's commentary with something positive. I wasn't even reframing my thoughts. All I was doing was *stopping* the spiral. And that alone was a win.

Then something powerful started to happen. The gaps between Darla's interruptions grew longer. Her voice faded a little more each time. The silence lasted longer, and in that silence, I started to feel strong again. For the first time, I realized I wasn't at the mercy of my mind. I had a choice. I had control.

That was the beginning of a whole new level of mental strength. And let me tell you, the difference between letting your mind run you versus *you* running your mind is so massive, it's almost impossible to put into words. It's like living in two different worlds... one where you're constantly under siege, and another where you finally feel free. I've put a lot of work into it, but now, Darla doesn't run my life. I do. And that shift has changed everything. I can still feel her try to creep in every once in a while, but my mental strength is strong AF now. I notice and send her packing before she even gets through the door.

I remember seeing a *Mad TV* skit with Bob Newhart that still makes me laugh every time I think about it. He's playing a therapist, and this woman comes in listing all the ridiculous things her mind does to her. She starts with, "I worry about being buried alive in a box." Bob listens, nods, and then says with total seriousness, "Well, stop it."

The woman looks shocked. "What do I do about it?" she asks.

"Stop it," he says again. "Stop thinking about being buried alive in a box. That's terrible."

I died laughing. The sketch goes on with her bringing up more and more irrational thoughts, and by the end Bob is practically yelling at her: "STOP IT! Just stop it! Don't do that anymore!"

That moment stuck with me. I thought, *Why not try this in real life?* Then my mind would start spinning, racing into dark, destructive territory, I'd literally say out loud, "Stop it." Not in a gentle whisper, either. Sometimes I had to bark it at myself like Bob Newhart yelling across the desk. It sounds silly, but it was the exact kind of visual and audio jolt I needed to break the pattern.

The stuff Darla was shouting in my head was every bit as irrational as that woman's fear of being buried alive in a box. Worrying about it, rehearsing it, criticizing myself over it… that was destructive mental behavior I didn't want running my life anymore. So, I gave myself a life hack: two words: "Stop it!" Every time I said it, I bought myself just a little more space between me and the spiral. And in that space, I finally had a chance to take my power back.

TRAIN YOUR BRAIN OR IT TRAINS YOU

Your mental strength is just like a muscle. It doesn't get strong by accident. It gets strong because you work it, again and again. At first, it feels clumsy, but with repetition, it becomes second nature. I practiced this everywhere, even in my car. I'd talk myself through the things I'd done wrong or the choices I regretted. Instead of spiraling into shame, I'd ask myself, *What was that for me? What did I learn from that experience?* It wasn't always comfortable, but it was real. And real was better than letting my brain just chew me up from the inside.

Our minds love to run wild, throwing out a million half-baked thoughts like popcorn in a microwave. Most of it isn't truth... it's noise. But because it comes from inside our heads, we treat it like fact. That's a big problem. So I started saying things out loud, right there in the car. Talk through it. Entertain Darla if you have to. "Okay, Darla, you think I can't do XYZ? Really? Let's pull out the receipts." Then I'd stack up the evidence—hard things I'd survived, tough situations I'd nailed, wins I'd earned. That was my proof. And when you slam the receipts down on the table, Darla doesn't stand a chance. She can't argue with facts.

This is where replacement comes in. You can't just shut Darla down and leave silence; you've got to swap her poison for fuel. Replace the negative self-talk with affirmations that actually empower you. And yes, I know affirmations can feel cheesy as hell at first. You'll say them and roll your eyes. It feels fake, like wearing clothes that don't fit. That's normal. You're trying to rewire patterns that have been running your whole life for years. Just because it feels unnatural doesn't mean it's wrong; it means you're doing something new. This will take practice and time, but you will see that the effort is well worth it.

Life Hack: Post-it notes. Cover your damn house with them if you need to. Write the things you wish you believed about yourself and put them where you can't avoid them: on mirrors, fridge doors, your steering wheel. At the beginning of this work, I should've bought stock in 3M for how many Post-its I had plastered around my life. It was

basically motivational wallpaper. I still use them, but now it's more strategic, no longer a full renovation project. Notes that remind you, *You've got this. You can do hard things. You're stronger than you think.*

RECLAIM THE POWER THAT WAS ALWAYS YOURS

The Big Guy upstairs only gave you one official assignment... don't screw up being you. Protect your energy and live in your truth. That's it. That's the gig. If you hand the wheel over to Darla, if you let her do the thinking, then you've completely shit the bed on your one job description from above. So stop outsourcing your worth to the clown on the toilet. If you'd give encouragement to your best friend, your kid, or someone you love, then for the love of all things holy, start giving it to yourself. You're listening, whether you realize it or not.

And part of not screwing up being you? It's learning to notice the chains you've been dragging without even realizing it. That's what limiting beliefs are—handcuffs you mistake for permanent. The wild part? They're not even locked. You could slip them off at any time. But wear them long enough and you forget they're optional. Most of these beliefs come from old programming, past experiences, or someone else's voice echoing in your head. They're not truth. But if you never challenge them, they keep you small, stuck, and living beneath your actual potential. The moment you call them out and set them down, you reclaim the power they've been stealing from you.

I wrestle with limiting beliefs every single day. I realized that I didn't just trip and fall into them. I was raised in them. I grew up in a strict, organized-religion household where limiting beliefs were literally *everywhere*. And they weren't even based on a God I could believe in. They were based on someone else's messed-up interpretation of God, loaded with a bunch of BS rules designed to control. A God that excluded you if you didn't check the right boxes. A God that handed out shame and guilt like candy, while the priests were diddling little boys behind the scenes. No, thank you. And yet, there I was, a forty-year-old woman, still following beliefs that had been indoctrinated into me decades earlier. Beliefs I never consciously chose. Beliefs that never even belonged to me in the first place. That realization was a gut punch.

So I started getting curious. My knee-jerk reaction in any situation was to assume *this is just how it is.* But then I'd pause and ask, *Is that really how I want to respond? Do I want to keep believing that?* Sometimes the answer was yes. But a lot of the time, the answer was, Hell no, *that doesn't land with me anymore.* Maybe it never did, and I just never took the time to examine it. When it didn't feel like my authentic self to me, in my knowing, I slipped off the handcuffs and set them down.

At first, I evaluated them one by one. But once I got deep into the work, really peeling back the layers, I started tossing limiting beliefs out by the dumptruck load. I didn't even need to analyze each one anymore. My gut was so in tune with who I actually am, beneath all the conditioning, that I could feel it instantly: does this belief resonate, or does it need to hit the road? If it didn't land with my truth, it was gone. No debate. No trial. Just straight to the curb. That alignment was powerful. It was the difference between cautiously removing handcuffs and shattering the lock with a sledgehammer.

Example: For years, I told myself, *I'm bad at remembering names.*

I said it so often it became part of my identity. It felt fixed, like a hardwired trait I just had to accept. But that wasn't the truth. It was a limiting belief. The more I repeated it, the less effort I put into actually improving. The truth? Remembering names is a skill, not a personality trait. Once I started using simple tools like association, repetition, and just being more present when meeting people, it got easier. Now I don't say I'm bad at names. I say, *I'm getting better at remembering names.* That tiny shift changed everything.

A big problem with limiting beliefs is how sneaky they are. Most of the time, you don't even notice them. They're running on autopilot, quietly dictating how you think, feel, and act. You don't stop to challenge them, so they set up camp in your mind like they own the place. But if you did pause, if you questioned whether those beliefs were actually yours or just something you inherited from your family, your church, or old wounds, it would be a total game changer. You'd get to decide which beliefs to keep and which ones to throw out with yesterday's trash.

If certain beliefs don't resonate with you anymore, change them. If you don't like how something in your life looks or feels, change it. You have that power. There is zero strength in victimhood. Every time you say, "Well, it's just the way I am," or "That's just how life works," you're handing over the keys. No one is taking your power… you're giving it away. STOP IT! Take it back. Own your choices, own your actions, and know that you always have the power to rewrite the story.

One of the best ways to build mental strength is to find small tricks to interrupt your negative thoughts. When you feel yourself spiraling into that dark loop, do something… anything, to break it. Light a candle. Take a few deep breaths. Say "Stop it" out loud. I've even clapped my hands as hard as I could and yelled "STOP IT!" like a crazy person in my own living room, because sometimes you need a shock to your system to snap out of the pattern. Honestly, what's more unhinged? Clapping your hands and yelling in your living room, or the fact that you've handed Darla the mic and let her direct the whole production... *your* production?

Try different things. Borrow from other people. Ask your trusted circle how they deal with that voice in their head. Better yet, admit to them that Darla is stomping around in your brain and see if they've met their own version. Maybe they don't know either, but maybe they'll start learning with you. Surround yourself with people who are also going all in on themselves, because the conversations you have with them will keep you stronger than trying to muscle it out alone. And honestly? Working with your people on leveling up is way more fun than watching the *Real Housewives,* aka middle schoolers in their forties and fifties who never made it past eighth grade emotionally. Yikes.

Mental strength is a slow build. In the beginning, it feels clumsy, like lifting weights you can barely pick up. Progress is hard to see at first. But if you pay attention to the small victories, those moments when Darla's voice gets quieter, when you bounce back quicker, when you choose a better thought, you'll start to feel fierce. That's the fuel that keeps you going. I've worked on this every day for years, and even now, I'm still improving. The growth I've made in mental strength is my favorite progress of all. Why? Because it pushed me. And that's exactly what makes it so rewarding.

Develop a mantra or affirmation that you can lean on when your mind starts sabotaging you. First, stop the spiral... then drop in the mantra. It doesn't matter what the words are, as long as they mean something to you. For me, it might be "I am strong. I am not the victim. I am claiming my power." For you, it might be "I am capable, and I choose to believe in myself." Write them on Post-it notes. Stick them on your mirror, your fridge, your dashboard.

Anywhere Darla likes to lurk. Yes, it feels cheesy at first. That's fine. Fake it until you make it. Every hack in this book will feel unnatural in the beginning. You've spent years letting your mind run you, so of course, it feels strange to flip the script. Do it anyway. I have the receipts that these concepts work... and what do you have to lose?!

Another way to build strength is to challenge your destructive thoughts with logic. Write them down, then reframe them into something neutral or positive. Don't let Darla give the monologue unopposed... talk back. Tell her to piss off. Remind yourself of the receipts, the data points, the evidence of everything you've already overcome. Pair that with compassion for yourself. A setback isn't proof you're failing... it's proof you're trying.

And that's the last piece: rewire how you see failure. Most people are terrified of it. Failure paralyzes them. They tiptoe through life, choosing the safe route, not because it's what they really want, but because it carries the lowest risk of looking stupid, being wrong, or falling flat. If you're not failing, you're not growing. If you're not failing, you're not pushing hard enough. If you're not failing, you're settling.

Failure is feedback. It's not a death sentence; it's data. Every "no," every mistake, every crash-and-burn is a map pointing you toward what *does* work. Some of the most successful people in the world are only standing on their mountain because they were willing to trip and face-plant a thousand times on the way up. You cannot shortcut your way to strength without walking through failure.

Think about it like the gym: Your muscles don't grow when you lift something light and easy. They grow when you push to the point of fatigue, when you risk wobbling and dropping the weight. That stress, which looks like weakness in the moment, is literally what makes you stronger. The same is true with your mental strength. Failure is the stress that builds your resilience. Without it, you're soft.

Some of my biggest breakthroughs came from flat-out screwing up. Times when I thought I'd ruined everything, only to realize later those so-called "failures" were just course corrections. They weren't the end of me; they were the path to me becoming who I actually am. Failure isn't the opposite of success; it's the toll you pay to get there.

So stop letting the fear of failure keep you frozen. Let it move you instead. Fail loudly. Fail publicly. Fail with your whole damn chest. Because failure means you were brave enough to show up. And if you can keep showing up, if you can learn to mine the gold from every misstep, you'll realize failure isn't the enemy... it's the most important ally you've got.

Theodore Roosevelt said it best in his famous *Man in the Arena* speech:

> *"It is not the critic who counts; not the man who points out how the strong man stumbles, or where the doer of deeds could have done them better. The credit belongs to the man who is actually in the arena, whose face is marred by dust and sweat and blood; who strives valiantly; who errs who comes short again and again, because there is no effort without error and shortcoming; but who does actually strive to do the deeds; who knows the great enthusiasms, the great devotions; who spends himself in a worthy cause; who at the best knows in the end the triumph of high achievement, and who at the worst, if he fails, at least fails while daring greatly, so that his place shall never be with those cold and timid souls who neither know victory nor defeat."*

That's it. The critics, including Darla, don't count. The perfectionists sitting on the sidelines don't count. What matters is that you're in the arena, face dirty, hands bloody, heart on fire. That's where strength is built. That's where real life happens.

CHALLENGE: MASTERING MENTAL STRENGTH

This isn't a one-week quick fix. Interrupting your inner critic is a practice you commit to every day, for as long as it takes, until Darla doesn't run your life anymore. This is training, and like any muscle, it gets stronger with repetition.

The goal is simple: catch her, shut her down, and replace the lie with truth.

Here's how:

1. **Catch Her.** Notice when the inner voice turns negative. It might whisper, *You're not doing enough,* or scream, *You always screw things up.* The second you hear it, you've caught Darla.
2. **Shut Her Down.** Interrupt the thought, out loud if you can. Say "Stop it." Clap your hands. Snap your fingers. Light a candle. Do something to break the loop. If you need a visual, go watch the Bob Newhart *Mad TV* skit on YouTube: *"Bob Newhart – STOP IT! The best two-word coaching you'll ever get..."* It's silly, but it's the perfect reminder that sometimes the most powerful tool really is just saying "Stop it!" When I say it, I literally visualize Bob in my head, and it makes me smile. If you put the right perspective on doing the work, it doesn't have to be torture. You can make it fun.
3. **Replace It.** Swap the lie for something solid and true, not fake-cheerful, but grounded. Try: *I'm doing the best I can.* Or, *I'm allowed to take up space.* Or, *I've failed before and survived, and I'll survive this too.* This is where you

bring out the receipts. Remind yourself of the real evidence that proves Darla wrong.

To take it deeper: Jot down what Darla said, how you shut her down, and what truth you replaced her with. Keep building your receipts. Over time, you'll have a whole archive of proof that Darla is full of shit and that you're stronger than you ever gave yourself credit for.

And remember: You don't have to believe everything you think. Especially not when it's Darla running her mouth. Failure isn't the enemy. Listening to her is. Fail forward. Fail loudly.

CHAPTER 7
JUDGMENT

Have you ever slowed down long enough to notice what judgment actually feels like on you... energetically? It doesn't matter if it's you judging yourself or judging someone else; it lands like slime on your mind, body, and spirit. Judgment is heavy, sticky, and gross. It doesn't feel good at all, so why are we all such experts at it? Because judgment grows out of insecurity and comparison. In today's culture, comparison is our favorite drug. We mainline it daily through social media, gossip, and side-eye glances. All it does is fan the flames of insecurity and prevent connection.

Judgment is everywhere. It's in the scroll, in the mirror, in the way we talk to each other. It gives off toxic vibes, whether we mean it to or not. At its root, judgment is fear: fear of not measuring up, fear of being different, fear of being wrong. It fosters narrow-minded thinking and feeds our limiting beliefs like fertilizer. Judgment isn't inevitable. You can reframe it. Instead of defaulting to judgment, you can shift into curiosity. Observe. Ask questions. Learn about yourself and others without making it a competition. Curiosity expands. Judgment shrinks.

Ever notice how often people judge themselves out loud the very first time you meet them? It's like they want to beat you to the punch... get the insult in before you can. That, to me, feels gross on both sides. I don't want to be put in the position of silently disagreeing with someone's self-criticism, and I don't want to watch someone shrink themselves before I've even had a chance to know them. But it happens all the time.

Here's an example: I run into someone I haven't seen in a while, and the very first thing out of her mouth is, "Ugh, I've put on a few pounds." Honestly? That wasn't even on my radar. But by calling herself out, she's anticipating judgment and trying to control it by saying it first. It's like a weird preemptive strike. Regardless of the reason, I want to say: "Stop doing that. Stop cutting yourself down before anyone else even gets a vote." And that goes for all of us.

The moment you feel yourself sliding into a place where you're ready to judge another human being, including and especially yourself, you're out of line. Period. We're all out of line when that happens. You don't know what that person walked through today, yesterday, or in the weeks leading up to right now. You don't know their fight. Their pain. Their story.

Listening to other people judge is one of the biggest turnoffs there is. The minute someone starts making cracks about someone's weight, their looks, their clothes, it just feels like cheap shots from the kiddie table. It doesn't make the other person look bad; it makes *you* look small and insecure. Every time I hear it, my respect for the person doing the judging drops like a rock.

Now, don't get me wrong, I'm not coming at this from a pedestal. I'm not perfect. I've judged. I've been judged. I've sat on all sides of that ugly table. Addressing my judgment over the last few years has been one of the most empowering things I've done...

not just for me, but for the people around me. It has completely shifted the energy I bring into relationships.

What I didn't realize until a few years ago was that my judgment of others was secondary to my judgment of myself. I was brutal in my own head, super critical, constantly running negative thoughts. And when you treat yourself like shit, it bleeds out. You start projecting that same lens onto everyone else. How could I possibly show grace to others when I wasn't even showing grace to myself? The work had to start as an inside job.

And that's where radical self-acceptance comes in. When you stop beating yourself up, something amazing happens… You stop needing to beat other people up, too. Acceptance kills judgment. Every ounce of energy you waste on judging others is Skittles down the drain. Think of it this way: every time you judge, you're basically dumping slime on yourself first, then splattering it on everyone else in the room. Gross. So, not only are you draining your energy bank, but you're spreading toxic vibes in the process. And the payoff? Absolute trash.

Judgment almost always has a sidekick: gossip. Fact: It's one of the most common, socially acceptable poisons out there. When we gossip, we're just sitting in judgment of others; only now we've dressed it up as "sharing" or "venting." Gossip is judgment with a megaphone. It creates a toxic mindset not just for us, but for the people we pull into it. We fertilize our minds with sludge when we gossip, then wonder why everything in our lives starts smelling rotten.

It doesn't just stay contained in the conversation; it clings. When you surround yourself with people who are constantly gossiping and judging, it gets on you like smoke from a bonfire. You leave the circle smelling like it, even if you didn't light the match. Stay in it long enough, and that negativity seeps into your skin until you're the one carrying it around. Over time, it doesn't just affect what you say about others; it warps who you are.

So ask yourself: *Who am I in my circle? Am I the one who throws a struggling friend under the bus, feeding the gossip machine with their pain?* Not a good look... it makes you part of the problem. Are you the one who stays silent, letting the toxicity roll on without objection? Silence is still consent, and that's not leadership. Or are you the one who draws the line and says, "Nope, not here, not today"? That's power. That's growth. That's the vibe.

I've been in all three of those roles. And without question, for the rest of my life, I choose to be the one who not only defends, but sets the tone. Not just refusing to gossip, but shutting it down before it has a chance to spread. Because let's call it what it is... gossip is low-vibe, basic bitch behavior. And we're here to level up.

That's why I take the initiative to set the tone when I walk into a new group. With me, you don't get gossip disguised as bonding. You get the hard conversations to your face and the compliments behind your back. If I've got something real to say, you'll hear it straight from me. And if you're not around? That's when I'll be bragging about you. That's the standard.

And here's the other side of it: When I meet people, if their vibe screams judgmental, gossipy, middle-school drama, I don't waste my time. Period. I have the tough conversation up front, before they ever get close to my circle. I tell them straight out: That behavior is cancer. It infects everyone, and it's not welcome here. Do I care that it might make me sound like a controlling lunatic? Not even a little. Because the group of women I've built around me depends on a safe space, and that space gets polluted the second you let middle schoolers in forty-year-old bodies start mucking it up.

NO MORE PETTY, ONLY PROGRESS

We need more hype girls. Imagine if women everywhere decided their job was to amplify their friends' wins, speak life into each other, and defend each other like their Skittles bank depended on it. Collectively, we could take a giant step up... together. But right now? Women are horrible to each other. Too often, it's middle school behavior in grown-ass bodies. Petty. Small. Self-sabotaging. That's why we're still fighting for a full seat at the table. We keep shrinking ourselves instead of elevating each other.

If your friends are gossiping to you about other women, I guarantee that as soon as you're not in the room, *you're* the one they're tearing down. Who needs friends like that? What a colossal waste of Skittles. No wonder women struggle to be taken seriously; we're bleeding out energy on toxic nonsense instead of channeling it into building something powerful. And you know who's watching? Men. They don't have to work hard to hold the "superior sex" card when we keep undercutting ourselves with this petty bullshit.

So, let's stop the middle school EQ. Let's elevate. Let's be the women who handle hard conversations directly and speak shout-outs and good vibes behind backs. Let's be the ones who hype, not tear down. Because when we quit wasting Skittles on gossip and judgment, we finally free up the energy to take our place, not just at the table, but at the head of it.

Why are we still living in a world where women play small, act like we're stuck in middle school, and pull baby-bitch moves instead of actually supporting each other? It's ridiculous. And you know what? Mom wasn't wrong when she said, "If you don't have anything nice to say, don't say anything at all." Simple. Timeless. Still true.

AND FELLAS...

Let's not pretend this is just a woman's problem. Guys have their own flavor of middle-school EQ. The locker-room gossip, the constant one-upping, the sarcasm that's really just insecurity in disguise—it's the same petty drain, just dressed in different clothes.

Real men hype their brothers up. They celebrate wins, hold each other accountable, and have the hard conversations face-to-face instead of hiding behind jokes or shit-talking. If your crew eggs you on just to watch you crash, that's not friendship—that's sabotage.

The same standard applies across the board: show up real, or don't show up at all. Because when men quit wasting Skittles on trash talk and fake bravado, they free up the energy to lead with strength, build real brotherhood, and actually make an impact.

Being in judgmental environments, where gossip and trash talk are the background music, wrecks your energy and twists how you see yourself. You've got to get honest about which areas of your life are contaminated with that vibe and either minimize your time there or reframe how you engage so you don't get pulled under with it.

Even if it's work gossip or a friend group where negativity is the norm, you always have a choice. You can literally opt out by saying, "You know what? I'm working on myself, and I don't need to get twisted up in judging others, so I'm going to sit this one out." Then watch how much lighter, clearer, and grounded you feel when you're not marinating in everybody else's toxic slime.

Sure, you might lose a few connections by stepping away from gossip and judgment, but maybe that's exactly what needs to happen. Dead weight falls off when you start rising.

We define our lives by where we put our attention. The thoughts you feed, the conversations you choose, the energy you allow... it all adds up. Whether you're fueling growth, love, and gratitude, or letting gossip and negativity drain you dry, it matters. Attention and energy are your most powerful resources. Protect them like they're gold, because when you do, you take your power back.

When you consciously choose where to invest those resources, you become the architect of your life. Every day, you decide the narrative, direct the path, and set the tone for what matters most to you. Attention is the gateway to your intentions, and your intentions shape the life you're living. It really is that simple... and that powerful.

Here's a reframe that changed everything for me: Instead of defaulting to judgment, try curiosity. Start with a simple line: "I want to come from a place of curiosity instead of judgment." Then notice what comes up. What's the data here? Why does this thing or this person bother me? And, this is the kicker: What does it reflect back about me?

For example, I used to get irrationally irritated with loud, over-the-top people in public. The kind who can't whisper to save their lives and suck all the oxygen out of a room. Then it hit me: *Oh, wait, that's me.* Loud, animated, extra. I was judging in them the very thing I had judged in myself. Once I reframed that, it was like a weight lifted. Those people didn't deserve my judgment. And I didn't deserve it either.

Everyone in your life is a mirror. Every single person reflects something back to you: your fears, your wounds, your growth, your potential. The things you admire in others? That's a mirror of what's alive in you. The things that make your skin crawl? Same deal. That irritation is pointing at an unhealed piece of yourself you'd rather not face.

That's why judgment is such a trap. When you're judging someone else, you're really holding up a mirror and yelling at your own reflection. You don't like their arrogance? Maybe it's because you haven't made peace with your own confidence. You don't like their loudness? Maybe it's because you've silenced your own voice. You don't like their "neediness"? Maybe it's because you've ignored your own needs for too long. Every judgment is data. It's not about them. It's about you!

When you shift from judgment to curiosity, those mirrors become tools instead of triggers. Instead of getting slimed with negativity, you get to ask, *What is this showing me about myself? Where's the work here?* That's how you grow. That's how you take your power back.

The mirror never lies. The question is whether you'll have the guts to look in it... and then do something with what you see.

Make no mistake: I'm not better or worse than anyone else. I'm me... a one-of-a-kind recipe. No one else has the same mix of ingredients, and no one ever will. Same goes for you. So stop wasting your Skittles on the comparison game. It's unwinnable. When you play it, everyone loses.

DON'T COMPARE, CELEBRATE DIFFERENCES

There is no comparison between you and anyone else. We're all on our own race, shaped by different experiences, struggles, and lessons. When you really let that sink in, everything shifts. You stop competing with others and start celebrating. You see differences not as threats, but as proof of the unique masterpiece each of us is.

When you let go of judgment and lean into curiosity, the world opens up. Everyone is carrying something you can't see. Everyone has a backstory. That awareness doesn't just make you more compassionate. It makes you free.

So run your own race. Let yesterday's version of you be your only competition. Reflect before assuming. Stay curious. Growth doesn't come from comparison. It comes from awareness, intention, and choosing a better response than the one before.

I'm reading a book right now by a woman writing about her body image and how brutal it's been to live under constant judgment. She's very overweight, and she shares what it feels like to be stared at, dismissed, and picked apart because of her body. And then she tells the story behind it: As a teenager, she was gang raped by older boys at her school. After that trauma, she did everything she could to make her body undesirable to protect herself from ever being seen as an object of desire again. Her weight became her armor, built from shame and pain.

Sit with that for a second. She was so hurt, so damaged, and yet the world still feels entitled to judge her body without knowing one shred of her story. And I can't help but ask: What kind of animals are we, sitting in judgment of people for how they look? For their weight? For anything? We have no idea what someone else has walked through. We have no idea what battles they're fighting just to get out of bed in the morning.

Flip the script: How would you like it if someone judged *you* with zero information? None of us wants that. But we do it to each other every single day. Judgment is lazy. It's cruel. And it's gross. And every single time you do it, you're throwing Skittles straight down the drain. You're draining your own energy bank while piling shame on top of someone else's pain.

If you find yourself in groups where gossip and judgment are the default setting, be the one who flips the switch. Redirect the conversation. Steer it away from tearing people down and toward something that builds instead of destroys. If you're not careful, you're not just participating in gossip; you're fertilizing the soil of shame and pain for someone else's story you don't even know.

If you're serious about leveling up, reference this book as your pivot point. Tell your circle, "I want to try something new. I'm going to work on eliminating judgment." Put it on the table as a group experiment. Even better, buy a copy of this book for the friends you care about most, the ones you actually want to rise with you. Imagine the shift if your whole circle committed to ditching judgment and gossip together. That's how we go from middle school EQ to grown-ass men and women leading the charge.

That shift can be incredibly powerful. You can take the lead in your group. Don't just quietly avoid judgment and gossip. Call it out, redirect it, flip it into something positive. Energy is contagious. If you're negative, people will catch it. But if you're positive? People will cling to that energy like oxygen.

So step up. Step into the role of a leader in your circle. Practice self-compassion as a way to quiet self-judgment. It changes everything. I've wrestled with compassion for myself and others for years, and it's still a work in progress. Judgment, both inward and outward, feeds off that lack of compassion. That's why I always encourage shifting into curiosity instead of criticism. Because curiosity cracks the door open for growth, while judgment slams it shut.

Reframing judgment is one of the most powerful skills you can develop. You can feel it instantly when others are judging you. It's heavy, defensive, suffocating. And the same is true in reverse. Nobody should have to defend themselves against your energy, whether you say it out loud or just think it in your head. Lead with understanding, not assumption. That's how you create space for connection instead of walls.

So next time you catch yourself judging, whether it's you or someone else, pause and get curious. Ask: *What's really going on here? Why does this bother me? Can I reframe this with grace instead?* That's the real test of strength. Because judgment is cheap, easy, and draining. Grace, compassion, and curiosity? That's leadership. That's power. That's how we level up.

Oh, and one more thing before we end the chapter with the Challenge. Here's a fun hack you can try, straight from one of the wisest women I know... my husband's second mom. She told me recently how she works on eliminating judgment in her own life, and it blew me away with how simple and beautiful it is.

She pictures humanity as a forest. Every single one of us is a tree, different shapes, sizes, branches, roots, quirks. Some are tall and elegant, some are knotted and wild, some lean sideways, some bloom, some shed. But all of us together? We make the forest. We're all connected.

So when she finds herself out in public and her brain starts drifting into judgment mode, side-eyeing someone who looks or acts different, she interrupts it with one word: "**tree**." That's it. Just "**tree**." A reset button for judgment.

It's so simple it's almost silly, but that's why it works. Because the second you say it, you remember: That person is just another tree in the forest. Different doesn't mean wrong or bad. Different means part of the whole.

Try it. Next time your inner critic pipes up about someone in line at Target, whisper "**tree**" in your head and see what shifts. It'll crack you up, calm you down, and pull you right back into curiosity instead of judgment.

CHALLENGE: NO GOSSIP, ALL HYPE

Most people gossip as a way to bond. No sugar coating: It's lazy, low-vibe connection that drains your Skittles and keeps you stuck in middle school energy. So here's your challenge: for the next thirty days, eliminate gossip. Zero tolerance.

When you catch yourself judging or gossiping, whether out loud or in your head, pause and reframe it with curiosity. Ask: *Why does this trigger me? What's really going on here?* Use the data to learn something about yourself instead of tearing someone else down. Or try the "**tree**" trick just to acknowledge when you notice yourself judging someone else. It interrupts the pattern.

Then flip the script. Behind someone's back, hype them up. Celebrate their wins. Talk about the good stuff. Save the hard conversations for their face, not the sidelines.

Notice what happens: your energy shifts, your connections deepen, and your Skittles stop getting torched on basic bitch behavior. Use them for building trust, leveling up your circle, and creating your best life. That's how you lead.

CHAPTER 8
STAY IN YOUR LANE

I live by a very simple concept that has created more peace and joy in my life than just about anything else: Stay in your own damn lane.

Now, don't let the simplicity fool you. It's harder than it sounds, especially if you're wired like me. Because for decades of my adult life, I was out there swerving all over the highway of life like a distracted teenager on a learner's permit. Someone else had drama? Boom! I was in their lane. Someone made a choice I didn't agree with? I was already halfway across the median to "fix it." A friend struggling? Step aside, I'll take the wheel.

I told myself I was being helpful. I told myself I was the best one to "handle it." In reality? I was stretching myself way too thin and bleeding Skittles everywhere. Picture one of those busted Pez dispensers, shooting candy all over the floor, except instead of Pez, it was my energy, my time, my peace.

Here's what I learned the hard way: Every time I left my lane to take on someone else's junk, I wasn't drawing from my overflow. I was scraping from my reserves. And that is a dangerous place to live. You cannot live a joyful, peaceful life when you're constantly in deficit mode, handing out Skittles like Halloween candy to people who didn't even knock on your door. When you keep giving from the bottom of your barrel, it builds resentment. The kind that simmers quietly because you don't want to admit you're burnt out. The kind that often goes unacknowledged until it finally explodes and comes out sideways: drinking too much, behaving out of character, or sabotaging the very relationships you care about most. Resentment is like mold. It grows in the dark, and if you don't deal with it, it will take over everything.

Resentment is tricky because it disguises itself as selflessness. You tell yourself you're being "helpful" or "generous," but underneath it, you're keeping score, even if you don't realize it. Every unacknowledged sacrifice, every time you said yes when you wanted to say no, every moment you carried weight that wasn't yours, adds another tally mark. And over time, that invisible scoreboard starts running the show. Resentment poisons connection because instead of giving freely, you're giving with a side of bitterness. Instead of loving openly, you're waiting for the other shoe to drop. Left unchecked, resentment eats away at joy, intimacy, and trust until there's nothing left but exhaustion and simmering anger.

I lived that cycle for years. I thought I was being a good wife, a good mom, a good human by doing it all: laundry, the kids' school and activities, the bills, the scheduling, the endless mental load of keeping a household running, in addition to managing just as big a career as my husband. I told myself I "had it handled." But behind the scenes? I was drowning in resentment. Every sock I folded felt heavier. Every forgotten permission slip felt like a personal betrayal. Every extra responsibility I silently picked up added another layer to the resentment pile. And instead of asking for help, I swallowed it until it oozed out sideways: snapping, nitpicking, sighing my way through conversations. That wasn't love. That wasn't generosity. That was martyrdom in disguise, and it was slowly rotting me from the inside out.

Resentment is a red flashing light. It's your mind, body, and spirit screaming that a boundary is missing. Instead of ignoring it or numbing it, use resentment as your signal. Ask yourself, *Where am I overgiving? Where am I saying yes when I desperately want to say no? Where do I need to put up a fence so I can stop bleeding Skittles everywhere?* The second you follow that signal and draw a clear boundary, the resentment loses its grip.

Looking back, I think part of why I was so eager to take on everyone else's issues was because it distracted me from my own. If I were elbow-deep in fixing their problems, then I didn't have to sit with my own discomfort. Sound familiar? It's a sneaky little coping mechanism... except it doesn't work. Because eventually, you wake up exhausted, resentful, and totally disconnected from your own lane, your gut, you... at your core—**you!**

That realization was my turning point. Once I saw the cost of carrying what wasn't mine, the only move left was to change and start choosing **me**.

STAY IN YOUR LANE TO FIND YOUR PEACE

The shift happened when I finally committed to staying in my own lane. Not half-assed, not "sometimes," but for real. And almost instantly, everything felt lighter. Peace. Joy. Clarity. The second I stopped wasting Skittles on problems that weren't mine to solve, it felt like dropping a fifty-pound backpack I didn't even realize I was carrying.

It was like finally fixing a leaky faucet that had been dripping all night in the background. You don't notice how maddening it was until the sound stops, and silence feels like heaven. Staying in my lane was all of that rolled into one giant exhale. For the first time, I had energy for what actually mattered: chasing my own victory, focusing on my own growth, and being fully present with my family, instead of half-alive from exhaustion.

But energy isn't a one-time win; it's something you have to keep protecting. The same way silence can get swallowed up by noise again, your focus can get hijacked the second you start looking outside your own lane.

Staying in my lane gave me the energy to actually run my own race. But it also made me see just how fast you can lose it. One of the biggest reasons? Comparison. The moment you start watching someone else's stride, you're already tripping over your own feet.

Comparison is one of the biggest culprits that yanks you out of your lane. The second you start looking left or right at what somebody else is doing, you've already drifted. The moment you compare yourself to someone else, everybody loses. You lose because you've left your alignment. They lose because you're not actually cheering for them, you're measuring yourself against them. It's a no-win game.

Blaze your own trail, from your lane. If you're in your lane, your only competition is yesterday's version of you. That's it. Nobody else. And that's where clarity, confidence, and momentum live.

Turns out, lane discipline isn't just for me; it's a whole-family game plan. My crew caught on quick, and now they love calling me out on it. My family has gotten so tuned in to this that "lane check" has become an actual phrase in our house. My kids love to call me out when they catch me drifting: "Mom, do a lane check!" And nine times out of ten, they're right. Ok... maybe ten out of ten... I've left my lane again. Sometimes I've gone so far out that I need Google Maps to get back. But honestly? I love that they're willing to hold me accountable. It's hilarious, and it helps keep me in check.

And here's something I've learned along the way: our families, especially our kids, are meant to be our teachers in this life. Somewhere along the way, we bought into the myth that being the adult means always being the authority, always knowing best. But what if part of our job is to set down the armor, drop the act of "having it all together," and actually let them teach us? That's not weakness, that's wisdom. Vulnerability creates connection. Authority alone creates distance.

Kids see things differently. They notice when you've drifted out of your lane, and they'll call you on it with no hesitation. They mirror back your blind spots, your contradictions, and your humanity. And if you let them, they'll keep you accountable in the most raw, beautiful ways. A child's perspective on the world is something we should all tune into more often. It's uncluttered, unjaded, and refreshingly honest. They see things in their purest form, without all the baggage and filters adults pile on.

I'll give you an example. My brother and his wife were explaining to their kids about a co-worker whose mom was in hospice. My sister-in-law tried to carefully explain what hospice was. My nephew, who was eight at the time, asked, "Why don't they just put them down?" (like you would with a sick dog). Before the adults could respond, my niece, twelve at the time, said, "No, we don't put them down—we let them suffer." Let that sink in. Disturbing, right? But also, brutally accurate. We wouldn't let our dog suffer the way we allow our sick and elderly to suffer. Out of the mouths of children comes the kind of unfiltered truth that makes you question everything.

So maybe the real flex isn't being the one who always "knows better." Maybe it's being humble enough to learn from the very people you thought you were here to teach.

Anyway, getting back to it... in your lane is really about boundaries. Without them, your life turns into one giant four-way stop with no rules, no signals, and everybody just honking at each other. Pure chaos. Once I figured out how to put up boundaries to protect my peace, I couldn't throw them up fast enough. I felt like a ninja, blocking out drama left and right, wondering how the hell I survived forty years without them.

It wasn't something that was modeled for me growing up. My mom was a martyr on steroids, and I thought that was normal. Looking back, it's no wonder my life completely blew out on my way to rehab. I had no fences, no lines, no limits. I was basically an open field where anyone could dump their junk.

It wasn't until I was a few years sober and supporting someone else at my "table of life" through their sobriety journey that boundaries finally hit me like a brick. I was at a support meeting in their rehab when the therapist facilitating the group said something that stopped me cold. He told us that if your boundaries are like Swiss cheese—aka full of holes—it's actually worse than having no boundaries at all. I sat there blinking, like, *What the hell is he talking about? Swiss cheese? Boundaries?* I had no idea what that even meant. *How is that possible?!*

The person I was supporting was one of my core tribe, so if boundaries were key to helping them, I knew I had to figure it out. That night, I started researching the best books on boundaries like I was cramming for finals in a class I didn't know I'd signed up for. One that I can't recommend highly enough is *Set Boundaries, Find Peace* by Nedra Glover Tawwab. That book cracked it wide open for me and gave me language and tools for something I had literally gone four decades without.

Boundaries are **everything**. At first, they were scary, because saying "no" felt selfish and foreign, but the more I practiced, the more my life improved. I realized I didn't have to accept every single thing people tried to pile on me. I could actually say no and still be a good person. (Wild concept, right?) Now I throw up boundaries like it's a sport and smile all the way to the bank with the extra Skittles I'm not wasting on other people's black holes.

Think of boundaries like hiring a badass bouncer for your life. You don't just let anyone waltz past the velvet rope and start drinking your good tequila. Some people get on the guest list, others stay out on the sidewalk where they belong. That's the job of a boundary. It decides who gets in, how long they stay, and how close they get to the VIP section of your energy.

When you don't have a bouncer? Chaos. Everyone's stomping around in your lane, spilling drinks, breaking furniture, and leaving you to clean up the mess. And you're wondering why you feel so drained.

Here's another way to picture it: Every time you say yes when you mean no, it's like punching another hole in your bucket. At first, you don't notice, but soon all your energy, the very Skittles you need to live, is leaking out. By the end of the day, you're bone dry, wondering where it all went. Boundaries are the patches. They stop the leaks and keep your Skittles where they belong: with you.

And then there's the classic: the oxygen mask. I used to think boundaries were selfish until I realized I was trying to save the whole damn plane without putting mine on first. Guess what? You can't resuscitate anybody if you're unconscious in the aisle. Boundaries aren't selfish; they're survival. They make sure you've got air in your lungs before you go running around trying to fix everyone else's turbulence.

So whether you picture your boundaries as a bouncer, a patched-up bucket, or an oxygen mask, the point is the same: without them, you're wrecked. With them, you've got the power, the energy, and the peace to run your own damn race, which includes being better for yourself, your partner, your family, your friends, your community, your employer, your everything.

And of course, as I started doing the work of putting boundaries in place, it wasn't perfect at first. I was clumsy. I started telling people, "I respect your boundaries. I respect your no's." And I meant it... mostly. My sister-in-law, Kaitlyn, whom I adore, would say no to me, and I'd grin and say, "I respect everyone's no—except yours." It's become a running family joke that I don't respect Kaitlyn's no. We laugh about it, but it just shows how awkward and funny it can feel when you're first learning to build that muscle.

Boundaries don't mean jack unless you communicate them. A boundary you keep in your head isn't a boundary; it's a wish. And people can't respect what they don't know about.

That's where the real work comes in: Say your boundaries out loud and then hold the line. Yes, it feels awkward at first. Yes, people might get uncomfortable. And yes, some will push back. But here's what you have to remember: If someone can't handle you saying "This is what I need," that's not a reflection of your worth. It's a reflection of their comfort with limits.

NO MEANS NO—FOR EVERYONE

The other side of this coin? Respecting other people's boundaries. This one is huge. Because if you expect your "no" to mean something, then their "no" has to mean something too. You don't get to be the boundary cop for your own lane and then plow through someone else's like it doesn't matter. That's how relationships crash.

I learned this one the hard way. Kaitlyn's "no" joke started out funny, but it also forced me to see the hypocrisy: how could I expect people to respect my boundaries if I was blowing right past theirs? That's the distinction; boundaries are a two-way street. You set and protect yours, and you honor theirs (obviously except Kaitlyn's) even when you don't agree, even when it's inconvenient, even when it feels silly. That's how trust is built.

So how do you actually start navigating this without turning into a controlling lunatic? Here are a few starter tips:

- **Be clear, not cloudy.** If you want someone to respect your boundary, say it directly. "I can't take calls after 9 p.m." works. "Wow, I get really tired sometimes" does not.
- **Start small.** Practice with low-stakes situations. Say no to an extra project at work or skip a social event you don't have energy for. Build the muscle.
- **Expect pushback.** Some people benefit from you having no boundaries. When you change, they'll notice, and not in a good way. Hold the line anyway.
- **Respect the "no."** Even if you don't agree with it, even if you don't like it. Other people's boundaries are about them, not you. The quickest way to show you're serious about your own is to prove you can honor someone else's... with the exception of Kaitlyn's, of course.
- **Repeat as needed.** Boundaries aren't a one-and-done. Sometimes you'll have to reinforce them. Think of it like training. Consistency matters.

Boundaries aren't about building walls; they're about building clarity. They create clean lines where resentment can't grow. They show people how to treat you, and they show you how to treat them. The better you get at this, the more peace you'll protect, the more Skittles you'll save, and the stronger your relationships will become.

If you're not sure where to even start with boundaries, let me help. They're not just for big dramatic moments. They show up in everyday life. Here are a few places where most of us need stronger ones:

- **Your time.** Saying no to commitments you don't have the energy for. Example: "Thanks for thinking of me, but I can't take that on right now."
- **Your space.** Shutting down people who pop by uninvited or overstay their welcome. Example: "I love seeing you, but tonight doesn't work."
- **Your work.** Drawing a line with bosses or coworkers who expect you to be available 24/7. Example: "I'll take care of that tomorrow during work hours."
- **Your family.** Pushing back when relatives comment on your body, your choices, or your parenting. Example: "I appreciate your concern, but I'm not open to feedback on that."
- **Your energy.** Saying no to conversations or environments that leave you drained, like gossip, conflict, or drama. Example: "I don't want to get into that, let's talk about something else."

Boundaries don't require an essay. In fact, the more words you add, the more cracks you leave for someone to climb through. Keep it short. Keep it clear. And if you're worried about sounding mean, remember this: clarity is kindness. Waffling is what breeds resentment for both sides.

Boundaries are everywhere once you start spotting them. The trick is to remember that every "yes" you give to someone else is a "no" to yourself unless it comes from overflow. Protect your lane, protect your peace, protect your Skittles.

Other people's opinions of you are none of your business. Read that again. **None.** If you're a person who camps out in the comment section, let me help you: STOP IT! Stop eating crumbs from strangers' opinions. They don't belong in your lane. You've got better things to do, like listening to your gut and focusing on what actually sparks your soul.

The world constantly entices us to drift: social media, politics, religion, gossip, everybody yelling about what's "right" or "wrong." What are we all doing? There's no prize for abandoning your lane. No medal. No reward. Only exhaustion and wasted energy. You're out there fighting battles for people who don't even matter in your life. And the Skittles meter just keeps ticking down.

A while back, I had a conversation with my dad that brought this home. He's pro-life. I'm pro-choice. Normally, that would've ended in a heated discussion, but this time, we talked calmly. He was explaining his perspective, and I simply asked, "Dad, how would you feel if someone came in and told Mom what she had to do about her breast cancer?" My mom's in her seventies; she's been through this before, and she's chosen not to go through chemo or surgery again. Without hesitation, my dad said, "That's her decision. I support her." Exactly. That's the point. Nobody else gets to make those calls. Stay in your lane.

That conversation showed me something: You don't have to convince people of your beliefs. You don't have to force yourself into their lane. You can simply invite curiosity. That's what I love: conversations that make me think, that challenge me, that give me a new perspective. Not to change me, but to stretch me. That's what happens when we stay in our own lanes and let others do the same.

Because at the end of the day, no one else fully understands your life, your choices, or the Skittles it cost you to get here. And it's not your place to dictate what anyone else does with theirs.

Imagine how different this world would feel if more of us just stayed in our lanes, focused on our own healing, growth, and progress, while respecting others to do the same.

So here's the life hack: Save your Skittles. Use them to fuel your own race instead of bleeding them out on other people's highways. Protect your lane like your peace depends on it... because it does.

Pattern Interrupt: Use the "lane check" life hack within your family or group of friends. Be willing not only to say the hard thing when you notice them out of their lane, but also be willing to receive, without being defensive, when they lane-check you.

Protecting your lane isn't just a metaphor; it's a daily grind. It sounds simple until you're living with people who know exactly how to weave into your lane, cut you off, and hit every emotional pothole on purpose. That's when I realized boundaries couldn't just be a concept I preached; they had to be a practice we lived. And like most of my best lessons, this one started at home with my kids.

For a time in my daughters' early twenties, my kids lived together in an apartment nearby. They weren't on the best of terms during that time, and they knew exactly how to push each other's buttons. Every conversation had the potential to escalate into a full-on showdown, and the tension spilled over into the whole family. It was exhausting for them, for me, for all of us. After watching this pattern play out again and again, I realized they didn't just need discipline; they needed boundaries they could actually practice in real time.

That's when I came up with one of my best parenting moves: the safe word.

Life Hack: To help establish boundaries, incorporate a family code word and make a pact that everyone will honor it. I ended up putting pen to paper and drafted a contract that everyone in the family signed. Our safe word is "triggerfish." If a conversation is getting heated, uncomfortable, or simply too much, anyone—me, my husband, or the kids—can say "triggerfish." The moment that word is spoken, the conversation ends. No debate, no negotiating, no dragging it out. It's done.

It sounds simple, but it works. My kids have always been masters at poking each other until someone breaks, but the safe word forces them to recognize and respect one another's limits. It teaches them that boundaries aren't just about protecting yourself; they're also about honoring the people you love. It's a lesson I want them carrying into adulthood, because knowing how to step back instead of blowing up is a skill most grown-ups still struggle with.

BOUNDARY SCRIPTS TO STEAL

When you're just starting out, boundaries can feel awkward as hell. So here are some word-for-word scripts you can borrow until your own voice kicks in:

Once you realize boundaries are a two-way street, the next step is figuring out how to actually say them out loud. This is where most people freeze. You know what you need, but when it comes time to saying it, your throat locks up, your palms sweat, and suddenly you're saying yes to something you wanted to scream no to.

That's why I want to give you a boundary script toolkit. Think of it like training wheels—you can lean on these until your own voice feels strong. And because not every situation calls for the same level of heat, I've broken them down into three tiers: PG (clear + kind), Spicy (bold + playful), and Spicy AF (savage + unapologetic).

Use whichever tier fits the situation and your comfort level. Over time, you'll naturally find your own rhythm.

At work (time boundary)

PG: "I'll handle that first thing tomorrow during work hours. I don't respond to emails after 6 p.m."

Spicy: "I'll get to that tomorrow. After 6, my laptop turns into a pumpkin."

Spicy AF: "If it's past 6 p.m., it can wait. I'm not donating free labor to the corporate overlords."

With family (body/appearance comments)

PG: "I know you mean well, but I'm not open to feedback on my body. Let's talk about something else."

Spicy: "I love you, but my body isn't open for public commentary. Change the subject."

Spicy AF: "Unless you're my doctor or my mirror, my body is none of your damn business."

With friends (energy boundary)

PG: "Thanks for inviting me, but I don't have the bandwidth this week. Let's plan for another time."

Spicy: "I adore you, but my energy tank is empty. Rain check so I can actually be fun instead of a zombie."

Spicy AF: "If I showed up right now, I'd be running on fumes and resenting you for it. Hard pass—I'll see you when I can actually enjoy it."

When someone pushes your "no"

PG: "I already said no, and I need you to respect that."
 Spicy: "I already said no. Respect it."
 Spicy AF: "No is a full sentence. I don't stutter."

When you need to say no kindly

PG: "I appreciate you thinking of me, but that doesn't work for me right now."
 Spicy: "Thanks for thinking of me, but I'm out this time. Keep me posted for the future."
 Spicy AF: "I love that you asked, but it's not happening. Consider this my polite no before I upgrade to blunt."

Pro Tip: Don't do this boundary thing in isolation. Talk with the people in your tribe—your partner, your kids, your friends, your coworkers—about what works for them. You'll be surprised at how many hacks and phrases others already use to protect their energy. We can (and should) learn from each other. In fact, consider this an open-book test: cheating off each other's papers is encouraged in this classroom. The goal isn't to reinvent the wheel, it's to get better at rolling with it.

CHALLENGE: PROTECT YOUR LANE

Audit your life for lane drift. Where are you wasting Skittles on things that aren't yours? Arguing with strangers on the internet? Binge-watching trash TV you don't even like? Overanalyzing someone else's Instagram highlight reel? Meddling in family drama? Gossiping? STOP IT! Every time you feel yourself veering into someone else's lane, do a "lane check." Snap yourself back and ask: *Does this belong to me? Is this my Skittles to spend?* If the answer's no, stay in your lane. Watch what happens to your peace, your energy, and your progress when you finally run your own damn race.

CHAPTER 9
THE CUP

Think of your life as a cup you carry around every single day. Inside that cup are your Skittles, your candy-coated units of energy. Every choice you make either adds Skittles in or drains them out. When the cup is full, you've got plenty to give: you're patient, focused, kind, even fun to be around. When it's empty, you're running on fumes, snapping at people, complaining about everything, and wondering why the hell everything feels so hard. And the cracks? Those are the leaks, the boundaries you didn't set, the sleep you skipped, the "yes" you gave when you should've said "no." Everyone has a cup full of Skittles. The real question is: Are you protecting yours, or are you letting them spill all over the floor like a busted vending machine?

The tricky part about the cup is that it doesn't refill itself. There's no magical fairy hovering over your head pouring Skittles back in just because you're "a good person" or because you've been working your ass off. Nope. If you don't make the intentional choice to pour into it, rest, boundaries, joy, stillness, laughter, play, nourishment, it stays empty. You can keep pretending you're fine, but your body, your mood, and everyone around you will eventually know the truth. Spoiler alert: the people closest to you can usually see your cracks before you do.

Think about it. How many times have you snapped at someone you love, and it had nothing to do with them? They asked you where the remote was, and suddenly you're on a soapbox giving a fiery speech about how nobody in this family ever puts things back where they belong. That wasn't about the remote. That was about your cup being wiped out, not a Skittle in sight. Empty cups don't whisper; they scream. And God help the poor soul who did misplace the ketchup.

Most of us don't just have a crack or two in our cup. We've got gaping holes. Some are old leaks from childhood conditioning, like that "be selfless" badge you've been wearing since third grade. Others are from toxic relationships, burnout, poor boundaries, or the fact that you've been running around like a human vending machine, spitting out Skittles every time someone presses your button. If you don't stop and patch those leaks, you'll keep giving until you're a walking shell, like one of those claw machine toys that looks cute on the outside but is full of nothing but cheap stuffing.

You cannot serve anyone well if you're serving from fumes. Martyrdom is not a flex. Nobody gets a medal for being the most exhausted person in the room. Nobody's handing out a sash that says *"Queen of Running Herself Into the Ground for Everybody Else."* (And if they did, would you even want it?)

So what does it actually look like to protect your cup? For me, it's been everything from learning to say no without apologizing, to recognizing that rest isn't laziness, to not saying yes to every shiny opportunity just because I *can*. It's me checking in daily: *Where's my energy? Where's my cup at?* Some days, I'm overflowing and can give generously. Other days, I'm at a quarter tank, and it's all I can do to protect the little bit I've got. Both are valid. Both are necessary.

I know the temptation to "just push through." I lived that life for decades. But pushing through on empty doesn't make you strong; it makes you brittle. And brittle things break. Protecting your cup isn't selfish; it's self-preservation. Because when your cup is full, your Skittles stay bright, your overflow blesses others, and you actually *want* to give. Not from obligation, but from abundance.

So check your cup. Is it chipped? Leaking? Empty? Overflowing? Be honest with yourself. Because pretending your cup is fine while it's actually a colander is like putting duct tape on a sinking boat. It might hold for a second, but eventually you're swimming.

FILL YOUR OWN DAMN CUP

Early on in my marriage, I remember feeling completely drained, like every last drop in my cup had been wrung out. I'd sit there exhausted, convinced that something was wrong with the people around me. I literally believed it was *their job* to keep me happy. If I wasn't happy, then clearly, they weren't doing their part. My husband probably felt like he had signed up for a lifelong performance review where his bonus depended on whether I smiled enough that week. Eventually, though, life slapped me with the truth: It wasn't his job, or anyone else's, to fill my cup. That responsibility was mine. Always was. Always will be. Turns out I'd been farming out my happiness like a janky contractor gig—when the whole damn time, it was an inside hustle only I could run.

Filling your cup will feel selfish at first, especially in marriage or parenting, when you're told that "true love" or "good motherhood" means giving until you're a husk of a human. The problem is, when you don't prioritize yourself, you end up running on empty, and empty cups don't love well. Instead, they resent. And resentment is basically relationship glitter: One tiny speck sneaks in, and suddenly it's stuck everywhere, blowing up fights about who forgot the laundry or who left crumbs on the counter. A heightened sense of self-awareness about your cup and energy reserves isn't just helpful; it's survival for your sanity *and* your marriage.

When I finally made the shift and started putting my own oxygen mask on first, I hated it. It felt shamefully selfish, like I was betraying my people. I was so conditioned to believe that "good wife, good mom, good human" meant *pour out until there's nothing left*. It took work, ugly, uncomfortable, ego-busting work, to rewire that belief. And at first, I tried to cheat. I thought, *Maybe I can patch this up with a little duct tape and hold it together. Plug the cracks, pour faster, push harder. Surely I can keep everyone happy and still survive.* Spoiler: you can't. You can't duct tape your way out of burnout.

Eventually, I realized I didn't need patchwork; I needed a full reset. My cup wasn't just chipped; it was basically a busted Solo cup at a frat party. Everything I poured in drained right back out, no matter how hard I tried. So I had to rebuild. Stronger walls. No leaks. And then I had to get really clear about the worth of what went inside. Because not everyone, and not everything, is Skittles-worthy. Some things don't get a Skittle. Some people don't either. And that's not cruel; it's clarity. The cup, the energy, the Skittles, it's all connected. That's how I finally learned to measure what I give and where it goes.

Doing self-care, the real kind, not just bubble baths and candles, makes deposits into your cup. It's anything that gives you energy, adds to your Skittles stash, and reminds you that you're more than just everybody else's problem-solver. The math is simple: When your cup is full, you have more to give. When it's empty, you have nothing to give. That's why the goal is to give from your overflow, not from a place of scarcity. Nobody thrives when you're scraping the bottom just to show up.

If your cup has holes in it, and be honest, most of us discover we're leaking somewhere, you're probably already living in resentment territory. That's the warning sign on the road to burnout. You can force yourself to give while empty, but only for so long. If you're not getting regular deposits into your cup, whether from yourself or from experiences that genuinely refill you, you'll always run at a deficit. And deficits don't just show up in your mood; they show up in your health, your relationships, and your ability to even recognize joy when it's in front of you.

Trying to manage life with a broken cup is like trying to win a marathon in flip-flops; it's possible to keep moving, but you're going to wreck yourself in the process. It's not sustainable. That's why the oxygen-mask analogy exists. It's not just something flight attendants say because it sounds good. It's an instruction manual for life. If you're not taking care of yourself first, you're not equipped to take care of anyone else.

Filling your cup isn't the endgame. The real growth comes when you model it. Your family, your kids, your team—they're watching you every single day. They're learning how to treat themselves by watching how you treat yourself. If they see you running on fumes, they'll assume that's normal. If they see you burning out, snapping, or pushing through until you collapse, they'll think that's what adulthood looks like. But when they see you protect your energy, set boundaries, and unapologetically refill your cup, you're giving them permission to do the same. You're teaching by example that self-care is essential.

Teaching your kids to care for their own cups isn't selfish; it's one of the most important gifts you can give them. It's a lesson in boundaries, self-respect, and emotional intelligence. It's how we stop repeating the cycles we grew up in, the ones that taught us to pour out until there's nothing left. When you show them how to protect their cup, you're not just raising kids; you're raising future adults who won't collapse under the same exhaustion and resentment we've wrestled with. You're handing them a skill set that will keep them whole.

I saw this play out with my son. Because he was the youngest, he got the best version of me when it came to teaching this stuff. He was nine when I got sober, which meant he got an age-appropriate, front-row seat to me peeling back all the layers and figuring myself out. As I learned about these concepts, I taught them to him in real time. I showed him how to check in with his own cup, how to see where his Skittles were at, and how to recognize that his happiness is his responsibility. Being in tune with your energy, your position with your own Skittles, isn't just nice to have; it's the difference between navigating life resentful and drained, or moving through it with clarity and strength. That's the gift I wanted him to leave home with.

When I finally committed to taking care of my cup, everything changed. At first, I felt like a selfish brat. Honestly, I had a full-on guilt hangover every time I chose myself over someone else's crisis. I'm actually *better* for everyone when I put myself first. The irony! What I thought was selfish was actually the most selfless thing I could do. Whether it was sneaking a book like it was contraband, hiding in my closet like it was a war bunker, or sitting in the car in the driveway just to remember who the hell I was. It all counted. It wasn't about spa weekends or dramatic life overhauls. It was about carving out tiny pockets of sanity. And sometimes those tiny pockets were the difference between "happy mom" and "burn-it-all-down mom."

Knowing what you need and then unapologetically taking the time, energy, and resources to meet those needs is everything.

That's when you finally start giving from your overflow instead of your scraps. And those Skittles? They hit different when they come from a full cup. They're softer, brighter, juicier... basically the Costco-sized variety pack instead of the gas-station reject bag. You give because you *want* to, not because you're obligated and running on fumes. And that shift? People can feel it.

Stabilizing your cup is non-negotiable. Patch the leaks. Monitor your Skittle supply like it's your retirement account. When you give from a steady, overflowing cup, it doesn't feel like a sacrifice anymore; it feels like generosity. And generosity is joy. That's the sweet spot: You feel good, they feel good, and nobody ends up burned out or bitter.

In my experience, Mom sets the tone for the household. If Mom's a frazzled tornado, whipping through the kitchen with her hair on fire, guess what? Everyone else feels the storm. But when she's grounded, clear, and giving from her overflow, the whole environment shifts. It's calmer. Lighter. Hell, even the dog seems less anxious. When you give from overflow, you're not offering up what you can't afford to lose. You're sharing the extra. And that? That's real power.

Energy isn't Monopoly money. You don't get to print more just because life demands it. When you're constantly running at an energy deficit, you *will* burn out. I know this because I've done it. I didn't just flirt with burnout; I full-on torched my life to the ground, and the wild part is, I didn't even see it happening. I thought I was "managing." In reality? I was scraping together crumbs, tossing scraps into a cracked cup that couldn't hold a damn thing.

An empty cup doesn't just affect *you*. It seeps into everything. Your relationships get thinner. Your work suffers. Your mental state nosedives. You turn into a hollowed-out version of yourself, operating from scarcity, fear, and lack. And nobody, absolutely nobody, was put on this earth just to white-knuckle their way through life as a shell of who they're meant to be.

And if none of this hits yet, let me give you the mic-drop reason: your kids can feel it. They're sponges. They know when you're tapped out, even if you're smiling through your teeth and saying, "I'm fine." And while so many parents love to say, "I'd do anything for my kids," let's be clear: being a martyr isn't noble. It's harmful. You don't just raise kids with your words; you raise them with your actions and the behavior you model. And if that example is self-sacrifice, burnout, and zero boundaries, guess what they'll carry forward? Yep, the same damn pattern. And then the cycle keeps spinning until someone finally calls bullshit and breaks it.

That's exactly what happened in my house. My three kids and my husband had gotten so used to me being a tornado that when I finally started patching my cup, it took them a minute to believe the new and improved version of Anne was here to stay. We had real conversations about it, how my full cup changed the energy in our home, how much lighter it felt, how much better I was for them and for myself. It wasn't just talk; I was showing them in real time how to protect their own cups. And you know what? It leveled up all of us. I'm the disruptor in my family. The black sheep. The one who's willing to say the stuff everyone else tiptoes around. That's my job. As I heal, my kids are watching. My husband's watching. Even our families of origin are watching. And by refusing to keep pouring from empty, I'm calling bullshit on the old patterns. I'm breaking the cycle.

Seeing the ripple effect in my own house made one thing painfully clear: This isn't just theory. A full cup changes everything. When you start showing up differently, the people around you can't help but feel it. The energy shifts. The tone softens. The whole system recalibrates. And if it can happen in my chaos-filled household, it can happen anywhere.

You don't have to accept exhaustion and resentment as your permanent address. You can start replenishing yourself by getting crystal clear on what actually matters to you. Not what Instagram says. Not what your mom thinks. Not what your boss demands. *You.* Prioritize those things like your life depends on it. It will look different for everyone. For me, it's time alone. It's learning, movement, investing in my mental, emotional, and physical health. Those things are non-negotiable. Why? Because I'm the most important person that I take care of.

Investing in yourself isn't complicated. It looks like doing things that make you feel alive. Bringing peace, joy, and fun back into your life instead of just trudging through it. Sometimes that means something small but wildly soul-sparking, like roller skating, shooting hoops at the park, signing up for that random dance class, or blasting your favorite playlist and turning your kitchen (or garage) into a concert hall. Don't underestimate the power of moving your body at 8 a.m. - whether that's shaking your ass, lifting heavy, or air-drumming like you're on tour. It beats starting your day with a headline about the world ending. Seriously, swap out the news for music tomorrow morning and watch how much lighter your whole day feels. Unless you're already one hundred percent in love with your life (and if you are, teach me your ways), it's time to shake it up.

You get to run your life. You're the driver, not the passenger. And if something isn't working? Change it. Don't wait for permission slips or divine lightning bolts. Just pivot. Because your life isn't meant to be a slow drip of "meh" until you die. It's meant to be lived: fully, joyfully, unapologetically.

Another powerful shift, the kind that rattles your whole system, is learning to say no without guilt. Especially for those of us wired as people-pleasers, this one feels like climbing Everest. We'll twist ourselves into pretzels, overcommit, and burn out just to avoid letting someone else down. And every time we do that, it's like punching a hole in our cup. The Skittles leak out fast, and suddenly we're running on empty. Meanwhile, we'll disappoint ourselves daily and call it normal. That's backwards. I lived by that belief for years, and now I look back and think: *Why the hell would I willingly betray myself just to keep someone else comfortable?* That's not noble. That's nonsense.

If something isn't aligned with your values or priorities, you're allowed to say no. Remember a yes to someone else is a no to you... wisely. You're allowed to save those Skittles for something that matters. Your cup doesn't refill itself—if you keep pouring it out for everyone else, don't be surprised when there's nothing left for you. Sure, maybe someone else will be disappointed. That disappointment belongs to *them*, not you. You were meant to take care of yourself first. You are the one person you're guaranteed to live with until the day you die. Trading your peace just to avoid someone else's possible disappointment, a disappointment you often can't even measure, because you don't truly know their expectations, is a terrible deal. Every time you choose them over you, you drift further from your gut, your intuition, your truth. Stop sabotaging yourself because you're worried about what other people think. At the end of the day, *you're the one who matters most.*

When I work with people on this, it takes practice. Saying no feels clunky at first, like wearing shoes that don't quite fit. But then come the breakthroughs—the little aha moments when they realize they're showing up better for everyone. Not out of guilt. Not out of obligation. But out of genuine abundance. Those moments are proof that protecting your energy doesn't just save you; it transforms how you show up for others.

Protecting your cup is the ultimate act of self-respect. If you keep handing out Skittles you don't have, the cup doesn't just stay empty—it cracks. So go ahead, give yourself permission. Say no.

Get curious about what happens when you stop handing out candy you don't have. Try it out. What do you have to lose? Maybe it's just the burnout, the resentment, and the twisted belief that you have to earn your worth through exhaustion.

And what do you have to gain?

Everything.

Because at the end of the day, *you're the one who matters most.*

CHALLENGE: PATCH THE DAMN CUP

For the next seven days, check in with yourself once a day and ask: *Where's my cup at?* Be brutally honest, overflowing, half-full, wiped out, or leaking like a busted Solo cup at a frat party.

Then track it. Write down one thing that added Skittles and one thing that drained the hell out of you. At the end of the week, look back. Those notes are basically your leak map. They'll show you exactly where you're hemorrhaging Skittles and what actually fills you back up.

Stop pretending you don't see it. If Instagram scrolling at midnight is draining you, quit acting shocked. If saying yes to every "urgent" work request leaves you hollow, stop being the office vending machine. Patch the damn cup. Protect your stash. You're not Willy Wonka, and your Skittles aren't up for grabs.

CHAPTER 10
SETTING YOURSELF UP FOR SUCCESS

One of the most valuable things you can do, in literally any area of your life, is set yourself up for success. That phrase might sound cliché, but trust me, it's not. It's a life hack disguised as common sense. And like most common sense? People don't use it nearly enough.

I've taught this concept to my kids, my employees, my friends, random strangers in the grocery line (okay, maybe not that far—but I *could*). You can modify any number of things in your environment or routine to stack the odds in your favor. It's not about discipline being some magical personality trait that other people have and you don't. It's about building little ramps instead of running headfirst into brick walls every day.

Let's make it practical:

- **Fitness discipline slipping?** Don't rely on 5 a.m. "new you" motivation. That guy hits snooze. Instead, sleep in your gym clothes. Put your tennis shoes at the bottom of your bed like loyal little soldiers waiting to escort you into battle. That way, the first decision of your morning is already made.
- **Can't get up with your alarm?** Stop lying to yourself. Put your phone across the room. That way, you have to launch yourself out of bed like a grumpy Olympic hurdler just to turn it off. You might grumble, but at least you're vertical.
- **Always late for work?** (*Hi, it's me, your excuse-making inner voice: Traffic was crazy. The dog needed extra cuddles.*) No. Set your alarm for ten minutes earlier. Boom, instant smoother mornings.
- **Life feels like chaos is your middle name?** Newsflash: "Chaotic mess" is not a birthright. You don't have to keep living like your schedule was set up by a drunk raccoon. You can shift this, starting now.

Here's an example from my life: My husband and I have *very* different ways of keeping life on track. I like to look a day, a week, a month ahead. Meanwhile, he's busy scanning 1–5 years into the future like some kind of long-range radar system. Sounds impressive, right? Except here's the catch: That zoomed-out planning has him saying "Oh shit!" more mornings than not because he forgot something happening today. Meanwhile, in my world? Very few "Oh shits." Why? Because I've shifted my perspective on how I engage with my life.

For me, it's as simple as taking a few minutes on Friday to "lay out my sneakers" for the week ahead, or on Sunday to glance at the upcoming calendar. If there's anything I need to prep so my week flows smoothly, I do it right then. That way, I'm coasting through my week instead of stubbing my toes and scraping my knees on rocks I could have easily sidestepped with way less effort. My husband's been saying his morning "Oh shits" for decades—it's not my pattern to fix. But I know which camp I'd rather be in.

Flip your mindset and start treating "setting yourself up for success" like a game. You stop being the victim of your routines and start being the architect of them.

Ask yourself:

- *How could I make this easier on myself?*
- *Where could I invest a few minutes now to save an hour and a headache later?*
- *What can I tweak so this task isn't a full-blown nightmare?*
- *What little shortcut would make me ten percent more likely to follow through?*

That's it. That's the game. Stack the deck in your favor and keep adjusting until you find what works.

HABITS MAKE OR BREAK YOU

Over the years, I've changed many habits to set myself up for success. Some were small things, and some were big things, but they were all deliberate changes that led to long-term transformation. I ask myself, *What am I lacking in this one specific area? What could I be doing that would make this easier?* It's worth putting energy into this because it drastically improves your quality of life. Don't keep dealing with the same annoyance week after week. If your life doesn't flow smoothly, figure out the appropriate life hack and make the change.

There's this thing my husband and I have both been doing for as long as we can remember. We call it "pimpin' projects," short for *Personal Improvement Projects*. These can be big or small, but essentially, they're habits or behaviors you want to change for whatever reason. When you notice something in your life you don't love, name it, make a plan, and start taking steps to improve it. Some pimpin' projects are quick wins, while others feel like they drag on forever. Either way, it's empowering to take charge of your life this way. Don't like something? Change it. Don't like the plan you made to change it? Change the plan. That's the beauty of it... in charge.

Here's a pimpin' example: For years, I wore exhaustion like a badge of honor. I'd brag about how little sleep I needed, then wonder why I was foggy, cranky, and running on fumes. Eventually, I decided, *nope, that's not who I want to be.* I declared, *I'm going to be someone who protects my rest like gold.* Then I set myself up for success. I researched what actually helps people sleep better—things like cutting screens before bed, keeping a consistent schedule, and creating a nighttime wind-down ritual—and I practiced them until they stuck. That became a pimpin' project I worked at until it shifted my whole energy game.

Another one? Mondays. I used to hate them. Mondays were the worst—weekend over, right back into the thick of things. But I realized I didn't *have* to keep dragging myself through every Monday like it was a punishment. So, I flipped it. I started telling myself, *This is a new start, the beginning of the week.* I started serving my brain fresh lines instead of stale excuses. And it worked. Now Mondays are my favorite day of the week. That's the power of reframing and setting yourself up for success with mindset alone.

The more advanced version of that pimpin' project, the Master

Level life hack, is when you unlock the ability to treat *every* day like it's worth celebrating. Tuesday holds the same enjoyment as Saturday. Wednesday doesn't feel like a slog. Sunday night doesn't come with that "back to the grind" pit in your stomach. That's when you know you've leveled up, you're not just playing the "make Mondays better" game anymore, you've beaten the boss level where all seven days carry equal value. That's one of the perks of doing the work: You stop living for the weekend and start enjoying the whole damn week.

And then there are the long-haul pimpin' projects, like my husband's culinary skills. He's been working on that one for years: experimenting, learning, tweaking, burning a few things along the way. But slowly, over time, he's gone from "hope you ordered backup pizza" to legitimately impressive in the kitchen. That's a pimpin' project with some delicious ROI.

Of course, not every project has to be life-changing. Some are tiny, but mighty. Like folding fitted sheets. For years, mine were just a wadded-up mess that made me feel low-key sad about my domestic skill level. Then one day, I got a life hack from a friend who suggested that I watch a quick YouTube video. I followed along and practiced a few times, and boom, I had it. Now every time I fold a fitted sheet, I get this ridiculous little smile on my face. Same sheet, same task, totally different energy. That's the magic of a mini pimpin' project: It doesn't just fix the thing; it shifts how you feel about yourself in the process.

Other mini pimpin' projects might look like:

- Finally mastering the TV remote so you're not pressing seventeen buttons just to get Netflix to load.
- Folding laundry the same day it comes out of the dryer instead of living out of the "clean heap."

- Putting your keys in the same damn place every time so you're not late playing hide-and-seek with yourself.
- Prepping tomorrow's coffee maker tonight so you wake up to liquid motivation on autopilot.
- Organizing that one junk drawer so you can find the scissors without an archeological dig.

They're small, sure, but every time you tackle one, it's like putting another Skittle in your energy bowl. Little deposits, little boosts, big ripple effects.

And then there are the *next-level* pimpin' projects—the ones that aren't about folding, cooking, or scheduling. They're about rewiring your mindset. Here's what I mean: Make your first reaction to anything solutions-based instead of excuses-based. Think about that. Instead of "Ugh, why me?" or "This is impossible," your knee-jerk response becomes, "Okay, what can I do to fix this?" That single switch can change your whole trajectory. Excuses keep you stuck, while solutions move you forward.

That's where the real power of pimpin' projects lives: The more you practice upgrading the small stuff, the easier it is to level up the big stuff, like your default reaction patterns. And once you've trained yourself to respond with solutions first, everything else in life gets smoother.

You aren't stuck playing the same old hand of cards you were dealt. Life isn't Vegas. There's no dealer standing over you saying, "Sorry, that's all you get. Good luck with your two of clubs and seven of spades." You get to trade them in, reshuffle, and ask for a new hand whenever you want. That's the beauty of being human. You're not trapped in yesterday's choices. You can shift gears, rewrite the rules, and make your life your own.

So if there's something in your world right now that feels off, change it. No big dramatic movie montage required, just a decision and a step forward. Take alcohol, for example. If you've started to realize it's not adding real value to your life, that's worth mindful consideration. You don't have to drink just because everyone around you is, or because people might think it's "weird" if you don't. Who cares? If they're that invested in whether you're holding a beer or a club soda, that's not your problem; it's theirs. Politely remind them to get back in their own lane.

And honestly, get curious about why someone else would even care. If someone asks why I don't drink, I don't launch into a TED Talk; I just flip the script and ask them why they do. It's amazing how fast that question flips the spotlight. For me, alcohol never actually brought value. Once I got honest about that, the decision became easy.

Here's where a pimpin' project approach really helps: Make a pros and cons list. No sugarcoating. No "but it's fun at parties!" excuses. Just a real look at what alcohol is bringing into your world versus what it's taking away. For most people, the cons list looks like it's been using steroids compared to the skimpy little pros column. And seeing that imbalance in black and white? That alone can spark some serious questions about the role alcohol plays in your life.

This isn't about preaching. I'm not here to tell you what to do. But I am here to encourage radical honesty and curiosity. Be real with yourself. If you don't like the answer you see on that page, that's your permission slip to make a shift. Trade the cards in. Deal yourself a new hand. And walk away knowing you've just leveled up.

Set yourself up for success by not sabotaging yourself in the first place. Sounds obvious, but you'd be amazed at how often people do the exact opposite. If you're trying to cut down on sweets, don't haul a Costco-sized pack of cookies into the house and then act surprised when they "mysteriously" vanish by Tuesday. That's not a lack of willpower; that's poor planning.

There are endless ways to set yourself up for success, but it all starts with this: You have the capability to change whatever it is about your life that you don't love. Read that again. You can change *anything*. Not everything all at once, not without effort, but anything you decide is worth the shift, you have the power to tackle. That's bold, I know, but bold is where the good stuff lives.

Preparation and mindfulness aren't just fluffy buzzwords. They're the secret sauce behind better daily outcomes. If you're constantly rushing, stressed out, and tripping over the same problems every day, that's not "just how life is." That's a systems problem. And guess what? Systems can be changed. Don't keep running the same day on repeat like some twisted Groundhog Day with worse snacks. If nothing changes, nothing changes.

When something doesn't work out, I'm not going to yell at myself to "try harder." Trying harder is exhausting. Instead, I ask, *What can I tweak so this flows better?* That's how you set things in motion. That's how you set yourself up for success. Plan ahead, create little systems, remove decision fatigue, and suddenly your efficiency skyrockets.

Sometimes the "small shifts" are the real power moves. Sleep, for example. If you're not getting good rest, maybe stop doomscrolling TikTok in bed until your phone literally smacks you in the face. Every doctor on the planet agrees: phones in bed = trash sleep. If you want to value sleep, put the phone down. If you don't? Fine. But just admit to yourself that you're *choosing* poor sleep. You're not setting yourself up for success.

So ask yourself: *What are the top three things I could improve right now that would change the game for me?* For me, it's water, sleep, and a consistent fitness routine. That's it. Nothing fancy, nothing complicated. But those three shifts make all the difference between feeling like I'm dragging myself through quicksand and feeling like I've got rocket fuel in the tank.

Next, figure out the little ways to set yourself up for success in those areas. Want better sleep? That might mean finally putting your phone down before bed. Radical, I know. Maybe you set it on the other side of the room so the alarm still works, but you're not glued to TikTok for the last hour of the night. Instead, you read a book. Boom. That one shift is massive. You sleep better, you learn something, and your brain isn't fried with blue light when you're trying to rest. All from one simple tweak. That's what I mean when I say "set yourself up for success."

Hydration is another one for me. I used to think, *yeah, I'll just "remember" to drink more water.* Spoiler: I didn't. So I had to hack it. For you, it might be setting a timer on your watch that buzzes every hour, or hauling around a comically large jug of water so you have zero excuses. Whatever works. The point isn't perfection; it's finding the little systems that nudge you toward success without you having to think so hard about it.

And if what you're doing right now isn't working? Stop repeating the same failure like it's some badge of honor. Don't shrug and say, "I'm just not good at that." Nope. Try something else. Then try something else again. We live in a time where you can literally Google *anything* and get more suggestions than you'll ever need. Type in "how to drink more water" or "how to sleep better," and the internet will hand you two hundred options in 0.4 seconds. Try one. If it doesn't work, move on to number two. Keep tweaking until you find what sticks.

Eventually, you'll catch yourself saying, "Wow, I feel so much better because I'm actually hydrated," or "I'm sharper because I'm finally sleeping," or "I feel strong because I'm moving my body consistently." That's not magic... momentum.

Once you know your top three, put your mental energy toward

them. Then align your actions with that intention. The real shift happens when your actions finally start matching your goals.

And let's cut the excuses. None of this "I just don't sleep well" or "I'm just not a water drinker." Sure, everyone has an off night now and then, but if poor sleep or bad habits are your norm, you're not just tired, you're bleeding Skittles all over the floor. And you're better than that. You're stronger than that.

If there's something I can do right now that takes one second but will save me ten minutes tomorrow, I do it. No debate. Five minutes before bed, I plan the next day. Sometimes that means reviewing my calendar so I don't get blindsided in the morning. Other times it's laying out what I'll need for meetings, scribbling a few sticky note reminders, or setting timers on my phone to keep the day on track. Even when I'm tired and don't feel like it, I still do it, because it's not just a task; it's an investment in tomorrow. And investments always pay dividends.

That small act of discipline means I'm not waking up scrambling, stressed, or running around like a chicken with my head cut off. I've already done the mental heavy lifting. I've likely saved myself thirty minutes of "oh shit" moments from things I would've forgotten. I've avoided unnecessary inefficiencies and created space for a smoother, more intentional, and actually enjoyable day.

Staying organized is huge. Organization keeps you in control instead of constantly chasing your tail. Being organized isn't about color-coded binders and Pinterest-perfect closets (though go for it if that's your jam). It's about buying back your peace of mind. The effort you put into it pays you back ten times because it gives you the power to shape how your life unfolds instead of letting life bulldoze you.

Discipline is another cornerstone of setting yourself up for success. Most people struggle with discipline because they see it as punishment, like a set of rules they "have" to follow. But discipline is actually an investment in yourself. You deserve to have goals, and you deserve to keep the promises you make to yourself above all else. When you see discipline as self-respect, as love for yourself, it becomes powerful. It becomes **huge**.

Picture the trade-off sitting right in front of you. On one side: "thirty extra minutes in bed." On the other: "feeling strong AF because I hauled myself to the gym." Which one do you want more? Pick one. You only get one. That's discipline... not emotional, it's math.

Too often, we let excuses and emotions muddy the water. We think, *I'm so tired. I don't want to. Ugh, blah blah blah...* STOP IT! Seriously. Stop it. Discipline is just a math problem. Either you want this, or you want that. Choose and own it. Love yourself enough to follow through on your goals.

Here's a fun example: My dentist told me for *decades* to use a water pick. And for decades, I ignored him. My excuse? "I don't have time." Which, let's be real, is not a valid excuse. You have time; you just haven't made it a priority. And that's fine, but don't lie to yourself about it. Be honest. Either it's important to you or it's not.

Finally, my dentist stated it like this: "If you don't start water picking, you're going to have adult gingivitis." I had no clue what that even meant, but it sounded terrible, so I decided it was time to stop half-assing it. My old approach clearly wasn't working, so I needed a new hack. First, I tried putting a calendar on the bathroom mirror to track the days I remembered. Didn't work. Next, I taped a photo of my dentist to the mirror so every night he could glare at me while I brushed. That one stuck. I could practically hear his voice: "Adult gingivitis..." and it made me laugh just enough to grab the damn water pick.

Now, when I'm exhausted and ready to crawl into bed, I ask myself: *Two minutes of comfort or adult gingivitis?* Easy math problem. And sure, sometimes I'll say, "Screw it, tonight I choose adult gingivitis," and then crawl into my cozy bed. And that's okay too, because I'm mindful and honest about it. Accountable to myself for my choices. No excuses, no stories. Just the truth. Excuses make weak people. And I'm not weak.

Another way my son and I set ourselves up for success: We choose "the chill way." It's our shorthand for making decisions that reduce stress instead of adding to it. If we're driving somewhere, the chill way means we don't pick the route guaranteed to give us road rage. We'd rather take the road less traveled, even if it adds a few minutes, because it sets us up for a smoother ride. The chill way feels like rolling the windows down, wind in your hair, sun on your face.

Compare that to the alternative: You leave five minutes late, you're stuck in traffic, you're swearing at strangers, and you roll into work frazzled and already playing catch-up. That's what happens when you don't set yourself up for success. The good news? You get to choose. You can always choose the chill way.

And the chill way doesn't have to be about driving. It can be applied to anything. It's about putting in a little extra effort up front so you're not struggling all the way through. It's about realizing you have the power to tweak things and choose a different way forward.

So get curious. Journal on it. Sit in the quiet and ask yourself: *Where could I choose the chill way? What small tweaks could I make to set myself up for less stress, more ease, more success?*

This doesn't have to be a solo mission either. Turn it into something fun. Bring your kids into it. Loop in your partner or a friend. Make it a challenge: *How can we set each other up for success?* When you flip the script like that, it stops being about constant effort and starts feeling like a game you can win together.

When you go all in on yourself, things change. Get curious

about everything—your logistics, your emotions, your mindset—and then set yourself up for success by making choices in the areas you *can* control. Those small investments, those small tweaks, those little life hacks, they add up. Suddenly, you're saying, "I used to suck at remembering names, and now I'm a boss at it," or, "I used to dread Mondays, and now they're my favorite."

Once you start seeing results, it fuels itself. You want to double down. You want to go harder because you realize you actually do have control over the quality of your life. No matter where you are right now, take control of what you *can* control. Set yourself up for success, and watch how much better life gets.

CHALLENGE: SOFTBALL + CHILL WAY COMBO

This week, I want you to throw yourself three softballs down the middle. Pick three things you normally trip over—mornings, meals, workouts, work chaos, whatever—and set them up to be stupid easy. Lay out your sneakers, prep your lunch, put your phone across the room at night, whatever your version is. Make the win impossible to miss.

Then, once a day, choose the *chill way.* That means looking at a decision and asking, *What would make this smoother, lighter, easier?* Maybe it's leaving five minutes earlier, maybe it's shutting the laptop at 9 p.m., maybe it's not answering that toxic text. Doesn't matter; just pick the road that reduces stress instead of adding to it.

At the end of the week, look back. Which softballs made the biggest difference? Where did the chill way save you the most Skittles? That's your roadmap. Double down on those. Because success isn't about grinding harder; it's about setting yourself up so the wins practically fall in your lap.

CONCLUSION

You've probably noticed by now that I don't do fluff, and I definitely don't hand out gold stars just for showing up. If you're here at the end, it's because you're serious about change. This conclusion isn't a pat on the back—it's your push to take what you've learned and run with it.

I've been reclaiming my energy and building a life that feels alive. Every Skittle I spent on healing, every choice to stay in my lane, has created momentum and results I never thought possible. The deeper I went, the more I realized this isn't just about me—when one person levels up, it sends ripples outward. Your family, your circle, your community all feel that vibration. Clarity is freedom, and when you strip away the masks and excuses, what's left is raw potential—and it's yours to claim. After years of doing the work, I can tell you this: real living tastes way better than stale crumbs. Once you've had the feast, you'll never go back to scraps.

Before the work, I wasn't living; I was numbing. It looked fine from the outside, maybe even fun. But compared to what's possible now? No contest. Once you've seen life in full color, you'll

CONCLUSION

never go back to black-and-white. That's all the evidence you need that the work is worth it.

Woo-woo doesn't have to mean chanting at the moon or buying out the crystal aisle. It can just mean saying, *I'm done with old shitty patterns. I'm curious about who I actually am.* For me, yeah, it includes tarot, stars, crystals, because they light me up. But the real woo-woo is getting back to the essence of Anne. The real woo-woo lies in peeling back the onion layers to remember who you are at your core, before life layered you up with all the things that dim your light. And that's available to you too... minus the Anne part.

Think back to when you were eight. Before you lost your innocence. Before numbing, before zombie scrolling, before Big Pharma, bottomless booze, or endless porn tabs. Before you compared yourself to everyone else. Before you loaded up the masks and judged everything and everyone, including yourself. Back when awe and wonder lived in your chest like a permanent campfire. If you had to choose between your yesterday on repeat or the wonder of that eight-year-old version of you, which would you pick? Exactly.

And that's what I'm chasing. I want the eight-year-old version of Anne to be proud. She'd see a woman who ran hard, fell down, got back up, and lived wide open: belly laughs, wild stories, scraped knees, detours-turned-adventures. And I want the eighty-year-old Anne to look back with tears of gratitude, not regret. Gratitude for scattering kindness like confetti, for choosing abundance over fear, for being brave enough to heal the parts that once felt unworthy, and then turning that mess into a message, living with intention, and leaving a massive positive impact on everything she touched.

Between those two Annes, little me and old me, is this one. Right now. Choosing. Daily.

CONCLUSION

For years, I thought I was the universe's duct tape: world-class chaos juggler, gold-medal fixer, my face on the Wheaties box: *Anne, Champion of Holding Shit Together.* I thought if I stopped, the walls of my house would literally collapse. When I finally stepped back? Nothing exploded. Nobody died. The walls stayed standing. The bills still got paid. The world kept spinning like it hadn't been depending on me the whole damn time. (Rude, honestly.)

That shattered the illusion of control. And in the rubble, I found clarity: My power isn't in duct-taping life together with Band-Aids and wishful thinking. It's in the choices I make.

Every day is a fork in the road. Stay or go. Speak or stay silent. Play safe or take the risk. Rest or run. Try again or tap out. Doing nothing? That's still a choice. Usually, the most expensive one.

Nobody on their deathbed ever said, "Damn, I wish I'd answered more emails." The top regrets are always the same: not living true, authentic lives, working too damn much, swallowing truth instead of speaking it, letting relationships fade, and never giving themselves permission to be happy.

THE WEB WE WEAVE TOGETHER

I picture living a true, authentic life to be like spinning a spiderweb. Every thread I spin when I choose to shine my light, whether it's love, positivity, or simply showing up as my authentic self, connects to someone else's thread. That one connection vibrates outward, touching not only the person in front of me but also the people they love, their families, their friends, their communities. My impact ripples, and then their impact ripples, until the web stretches farther than I could ever track or fathom.

That's the magic of this work. None of us operates in isolation; we're all part of an intricate web of influence. When you choose to shine instead of shrink, to spread love instead of bitterness, you set

CONCLUSION

off a chain reaction that you may never see the end of. One word, one smile, one choice to lift instead of tear down can travel through that web in ways that change lives you'll never even know about.

Imagine if we all did that. If each of us committed to shining our light, no matter how small it feels in the moment. Those threads would strengthen, the vibrations would multiply, and the web would glow with an unstoppable force of love and positivity. That's not some fluffy daydream; that's how change actually happens. One light at a time. One thread at a time. Until the whole world hums with the energy we choose to create.

So picture it: You're ninety, lying in that bed, the reel of your life playing. Is it beige PowerPoints and holding the peace at your own expense? Or is it a wild, messy, Technicolor montage of scraped knees, belly laughs, ugly cries, risks, boundaries, and love so big it spills out of you?

Don't wait until the reel is almost over.

Your eight-year-old self is watching. Your eighty-year-old self is rooting for you.

So here's your marching orders:

- Quit numbing yourself into a zombie.
- Shut down the doom-scroll and go live.
- Stop comparing yourself to everyone else.
- Drop the damn masks and the constant judgment.
- Say the hard thing. Take the scary step.
- Burn the script that says "play it safe" and write a new one that actually belongs to you.
- Live so fully that when the credits roll, people are standing on their seats, clapping like it was the best show they've ever seen.

CONCLUSION

FINAL WORD

Don't just go back to sitting on your couch, hoping for change. If you found life hacks in this book that you know will make a difference in your life, do something about it—for yourself and for the people you care about. Lend, gift, or suggest this book to family, friends, and other important people in your world.

When one person levels up, everyone feels it. But when a whole tribe levels up together? That's how you raise the collective. Growth isn't meant to stay private—it's meant to be paid forward. It's contagious, and every single one of us has the responsibility to spark it. Share the hacks, plant the seeds, pass the torch, and watch the ripple multiply.

If you like someone enough to buy them a drink at the bar... buy them a copy of this book instead, and share the hack that's been most powerful for you. Let's level up together—and then keep paying it forward.

ABOUT THE AUTHOR

Anne Karber is a tornado of ambition with a sprinkle of charm and a whole lot of heart. A fierce entrepreneur and unshakable optimist, she turns challenges into opportunities and setbacks into comebacks—all while keeping things wildly fun. She's the creator and host of *Let's Get Naked,* a passion project and podcast where real talk meets radical vulnerability, aiming to change the landscape by making authenticity the norm, not the exception. Whether she's building businesses or bold conversations, Anne brings contagious energy and a fearless drive to everything she touches. Buckle up, because when Anne's in the mix, things get real, raw, and seriously inspiring.

THANK YOU FOR READING MY BOOK!

Just to say thanks for buying and reading my book,
I would like to connect with you!

Scan the QR Code Here:

I appreciate your interest in my book and value your feedback
as it helps me improve future versions of this book. I would appreciate it
if you could leave your invaluable review on Amazon.com
with your feedback. Thank you!

www.ingramcontent.com/pod-product-compliance
Lightning Source LLC
Chambersburg PA
CBHW030247010526
44107CB00031B/1354/J